SAN FRANCISCO

LEGENDS, HEROES & HEARTTHROBS

WRITTEN BY DALE FEHRINGER
ILLUSTRATIONS BY JOHN MILESTONE

Dale Fehringer
2020

SAN FRANCISCO

LEGENDS, HEROES &
HEARTTHROBS

WRITTEN BY DALE FEHRINGER
ILLUSTRATIONS BY J. ARTHUR MILESTONE

ABOOKS
Alive Book Publishing

San Francisco
Legends, Heroes and Heartthrobs
Copyright © 2019 by Dale Fehringer
Illustrated by J. Arthur Milestone

Additional copies may be ordered from the publisher for educational, business, promotional or premium use. For information, contact ALIVE Book Publishing at: alivebookpublishing.com, or call (925) 837-7303.

ISBN 13
978-1-63132-075-0

ISBN 10
1-63132-075-0

Library of Congress Control Number: 201912345
Library of Congress Cataloging-in-Publication Data is available upon request.

First Edition

Published in the United States of America by ALIVE Book Publishing and ALIVE Publishing Group, imprints of Advanced Publishing LLC
3200 A Danville Blvd., Suite 204, Alamo, California 94507
alivebookpublishing.com

PRINTED IN THE UNITED STATES OF AMERICA

10 9 8 7 6 5 4 3 2 1

INTRODUCTION

One day if I do go to heaven ... I'll look around and say,
"It ain't bad, but it ain't San Francisco." —Herb Caen

From the top of San Francisco's Twin Peaks a remarkable vision lies before you. There are amazing views of the enchanting city below, especially on summer afternoons when a wispy, snow-white mantle of fog creeps over Twin Peaks, down the hills, and into the city, cooling kitchens and bedrooms in the Victorian houses below.

From that vantage, many of the city's historic treasures are visible: Coit Tower, the Pyramid Building, City Hall, the Ferry Building, and the beautiful bridges that connect it with the world.

Behind San Francisco's monuments are stories of the people who inspired them.

- **Joseph Strauss**, a tenacious and over-achieving San Franciscan raised funds for, designed, built and then wrote a poem about the Golden Gate Bridge.
- **Lillie Coit**, an eccentric woman from the bawdy Gold Rush days left funds to build Coit Tower atop Telegraph Hill.
- **Joe Alioto**, a charismatic and hard-driving San Francisco Mayor ramrodded approval to build the iconic Pyramid Building.
- **Willie Brown**, a colorful politician who ruled with style and panache was behind refurbishing and vitalizing the popular Ferry Building.
- **Friedel Klussmann**, a prominent member of San Francisco society, fought City Hall and was instrumental in saving San Francisco's famous cable cars.

Those are some of the legends, heroes, and heartthrobs who helped make San Francisco unique.

This book includes the stories of some of our favorite people of San Francisco. Each faced adversity with resilience, overcame a challenge, and accomplished something meaningful. And each left an indelible mark on San Francisco, the city they loved.

View of San Francisco from Sanchez Hill

TABLE OF CONTENTS

View of San Francisco from Twin Peaks

HISTORICAL SAN FRANCISCO PEOPLE

Every city has a distinctive nature, formed over time by individuals who stepped up, lived on the edge, and risked alienation to make a mark. San Francisco has had many such characters; each of them significant, and each unique. In the city's early days much of the population and most of the action were centered in the north end of the City: North Beach, Fisherman's Wharf, and Telegraph Hill. Today, that's where many visitors head first – to ride cable cars, visit Coit Tower, walk or cycle across the Golden Gate Bridge, and enjoy a coffee or meal at a North Beach café. Behind those attractions are stories of the people who helped shape the city.

LILLIE COIT

The Loves of Miss Lil

Coit Tower, which sits atop San Francisco's Telegraph Hill, is one of the most visible and well-known landmarks in the city. The woman responsible for it led a unique life that included three great loves.

Lillie Hitchcock, or "Miss Lil" as she was known, was seven when she moved with her parents to San Francisco. It was 1851 and the city was a rough-hewn gold rush town. One of a handful of children, she was treated like a princess, and spoiled by the soldiers and miners. She fell in love with the city.

As a teen, she saw a fire engine racing to a fire and ran to be part of it. The excitement enthralled her and she fell in love with the fire department. That upset her mother, Martha, who thought Lillie's behavior was beneath their status, and she sent Lillie away to boarding school. When back in San Francisco, Lillie resumed her relationship with the fire department, riding to fires and in parades aboard the Knickerbocker Number 5 fire engine. Firefighters took her as their mascot and gave her a badge with the number 5 on it.

As the daughter of wealthy parents, Lillie did what was expected of her, but she also engaged in less-accepted activities; including gambling, smoking, drinking, and dressing like a man.

An attractive young lady, Miss Lil had many beaus, but she fell for Howard Coit, a handsome and wealthy stockbroker who kissed her at a dance and pursued her. Martha didn't consider him worthy and demanded Lillie stop seeing him, so they were secretly married, which invoked Martha's wrath.

Miss Lil and her mother eventually reconciled, but Martha insisted that Howard was having affairs. He denied it, but Lillie couldn't shake her doubts, and she had a nervous breakdown. They lived apart until Howard died of a heart attack. He left his fortune to her, with a diary that declared "I love my wife better than all else on earth."

Lillie mourned him and went into seclusion. She spent the rest of her life grieving him, and she had no further interest in romance.

When she died (at age 86), her friends pinned the number 5 badge to Lillie's dress, and firemen served as honor guards at her funeral. In her will, she left funds to San Francisco that were used to build Coit Tower, a monument that will forever keep watch over the three great loves in her life.

EMPEROR NORTON

Don't Call It Frisco!

San Francisco in the 1850s was bursting with gold and silver miners, real estate speculators, Chinese immigrants, and sailors. It was also the home of America's first Emperor.

Joshua Norton was not always an Emperor. He started life in Scotland (and later South Africa) as an ordinary child, and he inherited $40,000 when his father died, which he used to sail to San Francisco and make a fortune in real estate and shipping. Among his associates, he had strong political opinions, and he often expressed a preference for monarchy over democracy, which spurred his nickname of "Emperor."

In 1853 Norton concocted a scheme to import rice from Peru to feed Chinese workers flooding into the city. But a glut of rice arrived, the price fell, and he lost most of his money. He fought to recover it, challenged lawsuits for lack of payment, sold his remaining assets, and declared bankruptcy. By 1856, he was financially ruined. He vanished for a time.

The stress of losing his fortune caused a nervous breakdown, and when Norton re-emerged, he was in an affected mental state.

On September 17, 1859, he walked into the offices of the *San Francisco Bulletin* and proclaimed himself "Emperor of the United Sates". (He later added "Protector of Mexico").

As Emperor, Norton attempted to find a resolution of the Civil War, ordered the dissolution of Congress and political parties, and called for a tunnel under the Bay and a bridge over it. He also forbade anyone to call his city "Frisco."

He roamed the streets dressed in a military jacket, beaver hat with ostrich plume, and wore a sword on his hip. He commented on the cleanliness of streets and inspected police uniforms. People loved him as a street character and gave him food, clothing, entrance to events, and paid his rent. Newspapers reported his antics, usually with a positive slant.

On January 8, 1880, the Emperor collapsed on a street corner and died. Thousands of people paid homage, and the *San Francisco Chronicle* declared "The King is Dead ... Norton I, by the grace of God, Emperor of the United States and Protector of Mexico, has departed this life."

Norton's legacy is kept alive by rituals in which people impersonate him, and he is honored on the anniversary of his death by an elaborate ceremony at his grave, south of San Francisco.

FRIEDEL KLUSSMANN

The Cable Car Lady

As one of San Francisco's most iconic landmarks, cable cars are popular with tourists and locals alike. Their rumbling wheels and clanging bells are as much a part of the city as the Golden Gate Bridge.

They nearly vanished in 1947 – victims of cost-cutting and modernization, and they were saved, in large part, because of one very special lady.

Friedel Klussmann, a prominent member of San Francisco society, was active in efforts to preserve the city she loved, and she fought for a beautiful and commercial-free San Francisco.

Her biggest battle was in 1947, when San Francisco mayor, Roger Lapham, tried to eliminate cable cars and replace them with diesel busses. The war had just ended and factories were ready to modernize the country. It looked like a "done deal," and Herb Caen weighed in, writing "the days of the cable car are numbered."

But Mayor Lapham and Herb Caen hadn't counted on Mrs. Klussmann.

On March 4, 1947, within earshot of the mayor's office, Klussmann convened leaders of local women's groups and formed the "Citizen's Committee to Save the Cable Cars."

For every reason to kill the cable cars they found a reason to keep them: they bring in more revenue than busses, are safer and more reliable, and work better in San Francisco's steep and narrow streets. But their most compelling argument was that cable cars bring tourists and income to the city; busses don't.

The dispute went back and forth with politicians, pundits, and residents discussing the pros and cons. *Life* magazine devoted several pages to it.

Klussmann and her allies obtained more than 50,000 signatures and demanded a charter amendment to keep the cable cars. A vote was held and the initiative won, overwhelmingly. It was a triumph for Klussmann, the committee, and San Francisco.

To mark her efforts, the cable car turnaround at Fisherman's Wharf is dedicated to her, and her story is told in the Cable Car Museum; fitting tributes to the Cable Car Lady, a resolute woman who used her power of persuasion to preserve one of the most popular San Francisco icons.

ADOLPH SUTRO

Building a Legend

He was an immigrant who used his creativity to amass a fortune. He then used his money to buy a big chunk of rapidly-expanding San Francisco, and he served as the first Jewish mayor of San Francisco. Through his efforts and generosity he enhanced the lives of everyday citizens, and in the process, he built a legend.

Born in Germany, Adolph Sutro was educated as a mining engineer. He moved to San Francisco to find his fortune in the Gold Rush, but instead, he operated tobacco stores, joined the Comstock silver rush in Nevada, and worked as a mill processor and engineer.

He spent more than a decade designing and drilling a tunnel that connected the Nevada silver mines, drained water, and eliminated gasses that were killing miners. He was paid a fortune for his efforts, and he got out at a good time.

Sutro returned to San Francisco and used his money to buy huge swaths of undeveloped land that at that time made up the western part of the city.

Always a builder, Sutro created a massive bath system (Sutro Baths) that held up to 10,000 people. He re-built the Cliff House restaurant and made it respectable. He constructed a mansion atop what is now known as Sutro Heights that had lavish gardens and the largest library in the western U.S. And he made the gardens and library available free to the public.

To help San Franciscans reach his properties, Sutro funded a railway that let them ride from down town to Sutro Heights, and he set the fare at half of what competitive lines were charging. His trains ran along the coast near Lands End, offering beautiful ocean views, and multitudes of San Franciscans rode his trains and enjoyed swimming in his pools, dining at his restaurant, strolling in his gardens and forest, and perusing his library.

Today, San Francisco has several landmarks that carry Sutro's name; including Sutro Heights District, Sutro Heights Park, Mount Sutro, and Sutro Tower. They are a fitting tribute to a man who built so many things for so many people.

JOSEPH STRAUSS

The Mighty Task is Done

Joseph Strauss was a tenacious man. Despite his small stature (just five-feet tall), he was an over-achiever driven to do great things, and as his signature achievement, the Golden Gate Bridge, attests, he was able to accomplish them.

As a boy, Strauss wanted to be a poet and an athlete. He wrote poetry his whole life and became reasonably good at it, but he was less successful as an athlete. While he was a student at the University of Cincinnati, he was so badly injured in a football game he spent time in an infirmary. His room overlooked a Cincinnati suspension bridge, which he admired so much he decided he wanted to build bridges. He did, dozens of them, including the Lefty O'Doul drawbridge across from San Francisco's Oracle ballpark.

But his most challenging project came when Michael O'Shaughnessy, San Francisco's city engineer, asked him to build a bridge between San Francisco and Marin County. Strauss agreed to the project, designed a gorgeous bridge, and fought for 10 years to obtain authorization and funding.

When the bridge was finally approved, Strauss took extraordinary measures to make sure it was done properly.

He ordered safety measures to protect bridge workers, and he made sure they were strictly enforced; including hard hats for workers, respirator masks for riveters, glare-free goggles, special hand and face cream, carefully formulated diets to fight dizziness, and an on-site field hospital. He required that all employees "tie-off" to the bridge to reduce falls, and he developed and installed a safety net under the bridge to catch workers who fell (and then became members of the "Halfway to Hell Club").

As a result of Strauss' concern and efforts, fatalities were well below norms for the time.

Strauss put his heart and soul into the Golden Gate Bridge, and his dogged efforts led to his death shortly after it was finished in 1937. He wrote the following poem to honor its completion.

The Mighty Task is Done

Written upon completion of the Golden Gate Bridge in May 1937

At last the mighty task is done;
Resplendent in the western sun
The Bridge looms mountain high;
Its titan piers grip ocean floor,
Its great steel arms link shore with shore,
Its towers pierce the sky.

On its broad decks in rightful pride,
The world in swift parade shall ride,
Throughout all time to be;
Beneath, fleet ships from every port,
Vast landlocked bay, historic fort,
And dwarfing all—the sea.

The Golden Gate Bridge

JAMES VAN NESS

A Square and a Street

San Francisco was a wild town during the Gold Rush. Practically overnight it filled with fortune-seeking adventurers who camped where they could, including in the city's open areas. One of those spaces, which early maps referred to simply as "Public Square," was a mess of sand dunes and weeds, which became filled with miners, tents, and trash.

In 1850, a newcomer arrived in San Francisco determined to improve the city. James Van Ness, an educated lawyer from Vermont, was elected to the city council, and he led a move to open the town's Western Addition section to residential development.

He drafted a decree (known as the Van Ness Ordinance) that directed the City Surveyor to lay out streets, and he ordered the land transferred to people who held land deeds. It also gave responsibility for developing the city's open spaces to the Park Commission, including the one surrounded by Post, Geary, Powell, and Stockton Streets.

Originally donated to the city by John Geary (the city's first mayor) the square was cleaned up in the 1850s. Squatters were removed, sand dunes leveled, and grass and trees planted. It was named Union Square during the Civil War, when it became the site of rallies to celebrate Union victories. At one point it included a huge pavilion, skating rink, and art gallery.

By 1880, Union Square had been transformed into a public park with diagonal paths, exotic plants, and trees. The city finally had a place for its citizens to relax, and over time it was surrounded by hotels and retail stores.

Van Ness was elected mayor of San Francisco in 1855. It was not a peaceful time, and the city experienced land disputes, corruption, crime, and vigilance committees. He left office after a year when San Francisco's city and county governments merged.

Although his stint as mayor was brief, Van Ness' efforts to improve San Francisco were significant. He helped the city expand, spurred development of a world-class plaza (Union Square), and had a major street (Van Ness Avenue) named for him.

ALMA SPRECKELS

She Got Her Sugar Daddy

Alma Spreckels spent a lifetime trying to influence the city she so badly wanted to accept her. In the process, the 19th century San Francisco heartthrob left behind several monuments and an enduring legend.

"Big" Alma knew what she wanted, and she went after it. She was a diamond in the rough, achieving her ambitions through determination, imagination, and sometimes just dumb luck.

Born in 1881 into a family with a father who claimed he was of royal heritage and didn't need to work, Alma de Bretteville dropped out of school to help her mother support the family. She studied art and used her wholesome beauty and well-sculptured body to find work as a model, posing (sometimes naked) for artists, and for the bronze statue atop the peace monument in Union Square.

She sought a rich husband, saying she would rather be an old man's darling than a young man's slave, and she succeeded when (after several years of effort) she talked Adolph Spreckels, a sugar baron, into marrying her. She took his name and spent his money.

Publically, Alma referred to her husband, who was 24 years her senior, as her "sugar daddy." When he died, she inherited a pile of money and became the richest woman in the West. Not generally accepted by San Francisco's high society, she threw lavish parties, donated to charities, drank and smoked, and cussed like a sailor.

Alma used her wealth to travel and build a villa in the north end of San Francisco that is still known as the Spreckels' Mansion. She loved art and wanted to appear sophisticated, so she bought sculptures and paintings and with her sugar daddy donated funds to build the Legion of Honor art museum that is still an attraction for locals and tourists.

Alma spent her later years in seclusion, donating to San Francisco causes, drinking pitchers of martinis, swimming in her private indoor pool, and mourning her declining social status.

Her taste in art had mirrored her affection for glitter, and her ambitions had exceeded her attainment. She had led the life she wanted, left a legacy to the city she loved, and above all else she got her sugar daddy.

San Francisco's Legion of Honor Museum

SAN FRANCISCO AND THE ARTS

San Francisco has been blessed with an abundance of artists, poets, and musicians – people who have made our lives richer. It might be the setting of the city, on the edge of the world, that attracts them, or it could be San Francisco's reputation as a creative center. Many of them struggled; some had troubled childhoods, while others fought poverty, rejection, and oppression. But they persevered and produced treasures for the rest of us to enjoy. They were driven by an inner force, which Maya Angelou described when she said "there's something which impels us to show our inner souls. The more courageous we are, the more we succeed in explaining what we know."

TONY BENNETT

Part of San Francisco

It would be hard to find people in San Francisco who haven't heard of Tony Bennett and can't sing at least part of *I Left My Heart in San Francisco*. It might be the city's favorite song.

Anthony Benedetto, or Tony Bennett as the world knows him, has sung the ballad hundreds of times: at historic events, the San Francisco Symphony Hall, and the Fairmont Hotel. It's his signature song, and it has helped him become part of San Francisco.

Bennett has had a passion for music his whole life. After his father died when he was a boy, he sang while waiting tables in New York City restaurants. He sang to troops in Europe during World War II. And he sang on the road for years, meeting and working with all sorts of musicians.

Throughout the ups-and-downs of his personal life, he has kept his music relevant to several generations of audiences.

During his long and brilliant career, the success of *I Left My Heart in San Francisco* has changed and guided him. He found it through a fluke.

In 1961, Bennett was in New York, preparing to go on the road to Hot Springs, Arkansas and San Francisco. Ralph Sharon, his pianist, was packing for the trip, and he noticed sheet music for songs that two aspiring songwriters, George Cory and Douglas Cross, had given him. One was *I Left My Heart in San Francisco*, in which the songwriters pined for their home town. Sharon took it on the trip.

After playing at a nightclub in Arkansas, Sharon took out the music, studied it, and decided he liked it. He called Bennett and they went through it together; Sharon played the melody while Bennett sang the lyrics. Bennett liked it, and so did a bartender working nearby.

"If you guys record that song," he told them, "I'll buy the first copy."

They performed it when they reached San Francisco's Fairmont Hotel, where it "went over like gang-busters."

Two local Columbia Record representatives were at rehearsal that afternoon and they thought the song had potential. Bennett recorded it and the public loved it, driving it to the top 20 songs in October, 1962.

Today, despite performing the song for years, Bennett still enjoys singing it, especially in San Francisco.

And, he adds, it has helped him become part of San Francisco.

Statue of Tony Bennett in front of the Fairmont Hotel

ANSEL ADAMS

Visualization

One of the best photographers of all time believed that really good photographs result from advanced planning and practiced execution – a process he called "visualization." Two events are involved: one external (in nature), the other internal (in your mind). You should see the picture internally first, he taught, and then use the camera to produce the equivalent.

Ansel Adams was born in 1902 in a house on the sand dunes of western San Francisco. He was a high-strung kid – gangly, nervous, and odd looking – with few friends. He entertained himself by playing the piano, became a skillful musician, and decided to make that his vocation.

As a teenager, Adams travelled to Yosemite with his parents, who gave him a Brownie camera. He fell in love with Yosemite ("there was light everywhere" he later said), with photography, and with Virginia Best, daughter of a Yosemite concessioner.

For years, he spent his summers photographing Yosemite, his winters honing his musical skills, and he pondered whether to pursue music or photography. Eventually, he chose photography and married Virginia. Both turned out to be good choices.

Adams spent years hiking and photographing Yosemite Valley, perfecting his art. Some photographs turned out better than others, and he occasionally became frustrated with his progress. Then, in the spring of 1927, he had a breakthrough.

After hiking to a strategic position to photograph Half Dome, he had materials left for just two more shots. He took one photo with a yellow filter, but then decided that wouldn't produce the image he had in mind. So for his final photo he switched to a red filter. The resulting photo turned out to be exactly what he wanted.

That, he decided, was the secret: pre-plan (or visualize) his photos, and then adjust the filters, exposure, and development to make it turn out that way.

From then on, Adams meticulously recorded camera settings for every photo, matched it with the result, and adjusted his future photographs to produce high-quality results. It turned out to be a revolutionary method of producing photographs.

Adams was lucky. He had a long and successful career, a wife who supported him, and the opportunity to work with some of the best photographers of his time.

He worked tirelessly, usually seven days a week, and wound up producing some of the best landscape photos of all time.

As he aged, Adams lobbied to preserve the lands he loved, taught photographic methods, and gave lectures and interviews to help pass his techniques to future generations of photographers.

When asked how he was able to produce such outstanding photographs, his answer was:

"The whole key lies very specifically in seeing it in the mind's eye, which we call visualization. The picture has to be there very clearly and decisively – and, if you have enough craft and have done your homework and practice, you can then make the photograph you desire."

Moon and Half Dome, Yosemite National Park, California, 1960
Photo by Ansel Adams

MAYA ANGELOU

The Importance of Courage

Maya Angelou was many things: singer, dancer, author, poet, philosopher, activist, teacher, mother, grandmother, and friend. She was also the first black streetcar conductor in San Francisco, at age 16.

She had a horrific childhood. She was raped when she was seven, and when she named the rapist he was murdered. She blamed herself, thinking her voice killed him, and she didn't speak for five years. Her mother supported her and told people she would talk when she was ready.

When she was 16, Angelou decided she wanted to be a street car operator. She liked the form-fitting jackets, the caps with bills, and the change belts. Her mother encouraged her to apply for the job, but when she went to get an application, they wouldn't give her one because she was black.

Her mother sent her back, and she went each day and sat, ignoring the racial slurs the secretaries directed at her. After two weeks, a manager came out of his office and asked why she was there. "I want to be a streetcar operator," she told him, "Because I like the uniforms, and I like people." She got the job.

Her mother woke her each morning and drove her to work and then followed in her car, to make sure no one bothered her.

At night, her mother quizzed her.

"What did you learn from your job?" her mother asked her.

"I learned that I like to work," Angelou answered.

"What else did you learn – about yourself?"

"I don't know," she admitted.

"You learned that you are strong, and determined, and you can go anywhere in the world."

She did, pushing through strife, loss, and racial inequality.

Shortly before her death she reflected on her life.

"Courage is the most important virtue," she decided. "Without it, you can do nothing."

Ruth Asawa

Good Comes Through Adversity

Ruth Asawa was one of California's most admired sculptors and the first Asian-American woman to achieve success in that field. But it wasn't easy.

Born in 1926 into a Japanese-American family in southern California, Asawa grew up in a life of adversity, both on her family's produce farm, where everyone did hard and dirty work, and in school, where she was looked down upon by some of her fellow students.

Three months after the Japanese attack at Pearl Harbor, when Asawa was 16, her father was taken away by FBI agents to a camp in New Mexico. Two months later, Ruth and the rest of her family were sent to the Santa Anita race track in Arcadia, California, where they were housed in a horse stall, and then sent to an internment camp in Arkansas.

They were confined with eight thousand other Japanese-Americans, including some animators from the Walt Disney Studios, who taught Ruth to draw. She spent much of her free time learning about and practicing art.

After 18 months, a Quaker organization obtained her release and helped get her into a college in Wisconsin, where she studied to become a teacher. After graduating, she was denied a teaching job because she was Japanese-American.

She attended Black Mountain College in North Carolina, where she studied art and fell in love with an architecture student named Albert Lanier. They moved to San Francisco, where they spent the rest of their lives, raising six children and pursuing their passions. Albert designed buildings while Ruth created sculptures, fountains, paintings, and wire hangings.

Over time, Asawa became renowned for her unique style of art, and most people associate her with her intricate wire sculptures. Today, several of them are displayed in San Francisco's de Young Museum.

Asawa was also a highly-regarded community leader in art education. She co-founded the Alvarado School Arts Workshop, served on the California Arts Council, the National Endowment for the Arts, and was a trustee of the Fine Arts Museums of San Francisco. And she started an art school in San Francisco that carries her name.

Despite adversity, she led a unique and inspirational life. She did her best, and she told everyone who would listen that she was not a victim, she was a survivor. Speaking of her experiences during World War II, she said:

"I hold no hostilities for what happened. I blame no one. I would not be who I am today had it not been for the Internment, and I like who I am. Sometimes good comes through adversity."

Ruth Asawa wire sculptures at the de Young Museum

MICHAEL TILSON THOMAS

It's About the Music

Michael Tilson Thomas, also known in San Francisco as MTT, is devoted to music. It's been the central focus of his life, and he loves to listen to it, study it, compose it, conduct it, and teach it.

Born in Los Angeles, MTT was a child prodigy. Much of his life, especially his musical life, was inspired by his grandparents, who were one of the most famous couples in New York City's Yiddish theater, and his father, a self-taught illustrator and musician, who despite being hearing-impaired was his greatest teacher.

His father taught him that the most important thing about music isn't how the music goes but where it takes you. And his father told him that only two things matter in music: what and how, which in classical music are inexhaustible.

He studied piano, composition, and conducting, and he worked with notable musicians including Stravinsky, Copland, and Bernstein. He studied at the University of Southern California, was Music Director of the Ojai Music Festival, and became conductor of the Boston Symphony Orchestra.

After directing symphonies in Buffalo, Los Angeles, New York, Miami Beach, and London, he took the baton at the San Francisco Symphony in 1995.

Tilson Thomas is devoted to musical education and diversity, and he brings new styles of music, composers, and variety to his concerts. For him, music provides connections to humanity and creates a new language that "speaks about who we really are."

His performances can be unusual for a symphony orchestra, and he has added jazz, rock, and pop to his concerts. He experiments with different types of music because he loves them all. He collaborates with the orchestra and shows them ways to make the most out of the music and each other.

For Tilson Thomas, the most important thing about music is where it takes you, as his father taught him. That might be a melody, a rhythm, an understanding of another person or culture, or what it's like to be alive. For him, life is not about ego or credit – it's about the music.

RICHARD SERRA

The Language of Art

On Stanford University's Palo Alto campus, near the Cantor's North Lawn, stands a huge, spiraling structure called *Sequence,* which consists of two enormous steel ellipses connected with an "S." Between the thirteen-foot-high walls a narrow circular alleyway tilts one direction, then another.

Surprisingly, as you pass through, you feel somewhat disoriented, but not uncomfortable. And when you reach the circular center you feel peaceful and calm, as though you belong there.

That would probably be fine with the sculptor, Richard Serra, a San Francisco native, who says the disorienting experience is because the piece "reverses itself right in the center … and you might have the concern that you're walking back in the same direction you came from, but you're not."

Serra wants people who walk through his pieces to feel good, and to have a relationship with space. He likes to open up art and let people walk into, around, and through them.

"Art teaches us to see in unforeseen ways," he has said. "The purpose of art is to make people think, to change meaning through perception."

Born in San Francisco, Serra has always loved art. He drew obsessively as a child, earning the admiration of his teachers and his mother, who introduced him not as Richard, but as Richard the Artist. His father, a pipefitter in San Francisco's shipyards, took him to boat launchings, where the boy saw massive steel vessels sink into the water and then slowly rise to float. That taught him that heavy objects can become light.

He studied at universities in Berkeley and Santa Barbara, and at Yale, and supported himself by working in steel mills and on steel buildings. He studied art in Florence, Paris, Rome and New York. He eventually shifted from painting to sculpting, and experimented with fiberglass, rubber, wood, and lead.

Ultimately, he settled on steel, and started doing large metal pieces in outdoor settings: torqued forms, arcs, spirals, and ellipses. He has installed his works in museums, businesses, and outdoor spaces all over the world. There are several Serra creations in San Francisco's Museum of Modern Art (MOMA), his piece, *Ballast,* graces the new UCSF Mission Bay campus, and his steel spiral, *Charlie Brown,* is installed at Gap Headquarters.

It takes an exceptional artist to describe the relationship between people and space. Serra is exceptional, and he is also determined, self-assured, and assertive. He shrugs off criticism and says he wants to be respected for his work, not his personality.

And he wants to be remembered for helping the rest of us understand a little more about the language of art.

*Richard Serra's Sequence, located On
Stanford University's Palo Alto campus.*

MICHAEL DE YOUNG

The Power of Information

As the dominant source of information in the 1800s, newspapers were powerful influences in everyday life. The people who ran the papers often wielded that power to their advantage. Such was the case with city pioneer Michael de Young.

Born in Louisiana, Michael and his family moved to San Francisco in 1854, in the midst of explosive growth that followed the Gold Rush. As teenagers, he and his brother Charles borrowed $20 and used it to start a daily bulletin called the *Dramatic Chronicle* that focused on San Francisco theater. Michael was the business manager; Charles the editor.

They distributed their bulletin, which included information on theater performances, by hand to patrons of restaurants, saloons, and theaters. The paper eked by. Then they got a break.

By a stroke of luck (19-year-old Michael happened to be in the telegraph office when the news came in), the brothers were the first in San Francisco to report the assassination of Abraham Lincoln. They rushed out a special edition with the story on the front page, and got a "scoop" on the other local newspapers. As a result, their reputation grew, more people bought their newspapers, and their advertising increased. They expanded the bulletin into a full length newspaper and renamed it the *San Francisco Chronicle*.

Charles was shot and killed by the son of a politician the paper had criticized, and Michael assumed all aspects of running the paper. Over time he turned it into the most influential in San Francisco.

As he aged, Michael used the newspaper to advance his interests and to gain publicity for his community activities, which included chairing the California Midwinter Exposition in 1894.

Fairs were big deals in those days, and de Young did a good job, including having funds left over, which he used to establish the first fine arts museum in California. He named it the de Young Museum and donated numerous items to it, including precious stones from Tiffany & Company.

As head of the most influential newspaper in San Francisco, de Young became one of the most prominent people in the city. He used his power to enter politics, including election as a city commissioner and serving as a delegate to three Republican National Conventions.

De Young and his wife, Katherine, had five children. Their only son died in a fishing accident, but their daughters and their husbands helped manage the *San Francisco Chronicle* until it was sold to the Hearst Corporation in 2000.

After a full and eventful life, de Young died in 1925 at age 75. He had no regrets, having lived the American Dream, starting with nothing and becoming somebody. In his case, he did it by understanding and leveraging the power of information.

The de Young Museum in Golden Gate Park

San Francisco's City Hall

SAN FRANCISCO POLITICOS

So much history has been made at San Francisco's beautiful Beaux-Arts City Hall. Twice damaged and rebuilt, it stands today at the center of the city and serves as a place where San Francisco comes to debate, protest, celebrate, and grieve. It has seen presidents, kings, soldiers and vagrants. Parades have passed by: anti-war protests, Gay Freedom marches, and victory celebrations. Champagne has been spilled there, as has blood. There have been many firsts there, too: the first female mayor, first African-American mayor, first openly-gay elected official, and first Asian-American mayor – each adding another page to the history of a splendid building and a remarkable city.

"SUNNY JIM" ROLPH

A Self-Made Man

High on the top of Sanchez Hill, in San Francisco's Noe Valley neighborhood, sits a house with excellent views and an interesting history. It offers a legacy from an old-time San Francisco politico.

"Sunny Jim" Rolph was a self-made man. He entered the shipping business, worked hard, and became rich and powerful. He ran for mayor in 1911 with a campaign that included fist fights, egg-throwing, and riots. He won and held that office for 19 years – the longest stint in city history.

Mayor Rolph expanded the Municipal Railway, backed the Twin Peaks tunnel to open the western part of the city, and led efforts to re-build City Hall following the 1906 earthquake.

He was a "sunny" man-about-town with a friendly disposition and clothes for every occasion: expensive suits, cowboy boots, even an Indian headdress.

Rolph built a mansion on Sanchez Hill, which some people called the "Pleasure Palace," that included ostrich skin floors, redwood rafters, and a fireplace built with stones from Yosemite's Hetch Hetchy Valley. It housed the mayor's mistress and many of his hard-drinking parties.

He successfully ran for California governor and took office in 1931. While in office he established the State Park System and instituted the first state sales tax, which some people called "Pennies for Jimmy."

A recall movement was launched in 1933; the same year a San Jose vigilante group pulled two suspected kidnappers from jail and hanged them. Rolph condoned the lynching, saying justice had been served. The press roasted him and he became known as "Governor Lynch." That did him in, and Rolph suffered a heart attack and died six months later. His body was brought home to lie in state in San Francisco City Hall.

Now all that is left of "Sunny Jim" is the legend of an eccentric mayor during a colorful period in San Francisco history, and a beautiful house on the top of Sanchez Hill.

JOE ALIOTO

A Beautiful Building

Joe Alioto had a full and interesting life during which he achieved wealth and success. He was also partly responsible for one of San Francisco's most distinctive buildings.

Born into an Italian immigrant fishing family, Alioto attended local schools, earned a law degree, and practiced antitrust law – first for the U.S. government, and later for himself. He represented big clients like Walt Disney and Samuel Goldwyn and his work made him wealthy and introduced him to San Francisco's movers and shakers.

In 1967, Alioto was campaign finance chair for a San Francisco mayoral candidate who died. Alioto stepped in, ran in his place, and won, and then was re-elected four years later.

The late 60s and early 70s were a time of upheaval in San Francisco, including the Summer of Love, the Viet Nam War, and the Black Panthers. Mayor Alioto's 0=response to those and all issues was energetic and tough.

He was widely-respected, but was also accused of being too harsh on protestors and the gay population.

Alioto was behind a 1970s building boom in San Francisco, and he supported construction of several high-rise office buildings, including the Embarcadero Center.

He also favored constructing the Pyramid Building, which was initially opposed by city planners, preservationists, and others.

The design, a triangle that tapered to a point, was controversial. Opponents called it a "dunce cap" and some people disliked the proposed height, which was taller than all of San Francisco's hills.

But Alioto believed in it and fought the criticism. He got the architects to reduce the height, and he forced it through the Planning Commission, threatening to fire them if they didn't approve it.

The building Alioto argued for is now a civic icon, giving San Francisco's skyline a unique and beautiful character.

As usual, Alioto was frank about how it turned out. "What the hell?" he said in a 1996 interview, "It's a beautiful building."

WILLIE BROWN

Da Mayor's Inauguration

Willie Brown, also known as "Da Mayor," ruled San Francisco during an extraordinary period: the dot-com era, the post-9/11 world, a housing crunch, soaring home prices, war protests, and scandals. He handled challenges with confidence, imagined things on a grand scale, and carried out many of them.

His administration restored City Hall (after the 1989 earthquake), refurbished the Ferry Building (turning it into a major San Francisco attraction), drove development of the Mission Bay biotech center, and supported a new baseball stadium. He appointed minorities to political positions: African-Americans, Asian-Americans, women, Latinos, gays and lesbians – more than any previous mayor.

He also threw the grandest inaugural party in San Francisco history. The event was open to the entire city, with seventy restaurants donating food, a soup kitchen to feed thousands of homeless and low-income people, and big name bands to play music.

On inaugural morning, January 8, 1996, Da Mayor, a real Clothes Horse, wore a dark single-breasted suit, mustard-colored tie, and fedora. The day began at St. Patrick's Church where clergy from various religions read prayers and commended him. As he left the church, police cleared a path, moving people aside so Brown could get across the street to Yerba Buena Gardens.

A crowd of 7,500 stood in the cold, windy fog to witness the event. Dignitaries in attendance included Dianne Feinstein, Barbara Boxer, Jesse Jackson, every living ex-mayor of San Francisco, and several legislators.

During the inaugural ceremony Brown took a telephone call from President Bill Clinton, which was broadcast to the crowd. The connection was delayed. "They've put me on hold! What nerve!" Brown told the audience, to roars of laughter. "I've never waited this long for anybody."

When Clinton came on the phone, Brown told him: "You should be here with us. There's no snow and no Republicans." And with that, San Francisco threw a blow-out party for 100,000 of Da Mayor's closest friends.

GEORGE MOSCONE

An Extraordinary City

Ask San Franciscans what they know about George Moscone, and they might say the convention center is named after him. They might also know that he was mayor, and that he was assassinated. Beyond that, there's little recollection of the man who helped shape San Francisco into an extraordinary city.

Raised in San Francisco, Moscone earned a degree at College of the Pacific, where he befriended John Burton, a future influential politician. He graduated from law school at Hastings College of the Law, where he met Willie Brown, another future politician. Both encouraged him to enter politics.

Moscone did, and he was elected to California's Senate, where he served with Burton and Brown and was named majority leader. He was elected mayor of San Francisco in 1975, and he appointed people to boards and commissions who had largely been excluded: women, gays, lesbians, Blacks, Latinos, and Asians.

He was in the midst of creating a new, more open city when he received word that Dan White, a city supervisor who had resigned, wanted his position back. White approached Moscone in the mayor's City Hall office and asked to be reappointed. Moscone refused. White shot him to death, then went down the hall and shot Harvey Milk. The assassinations tore San Francisco apart.

Dianne Feinstein succeeded him, retained his diverse government, and calmed the city.

Moscone left a mark on San Francisco, and in tribute several landmarks are named after him — the convention center, an elementary school, and a North Beach playground. And a statue of him in City Hall is inscribed with his words:

"San Francisco is an extraordinary city, because its people have learned to live together with one another, to respect each other, and to work with each other for the future of their community.

That's the strength and beauty of this city — it's the reason why the citizens who live here are the luckiest people in the world."

HARVEY MILK

Give Them Hope

Harvey Milk was perhaps the most influential gay man of the 20th century. He tore down barriers, earned respect for gay rights, stood up for the oppressed, and fought for minorities. Today, he is remembered for many things, but he would probably be most honored to be known for giving people hope.

After growing up in New York and serving in the Navy, Milk moved to and opened a camera store in San Francisco's Castro District. The store became a gathering place where Milk established friendships and connections and declared his candidacy for the San Francisco Board of Supervisors.

Milk was a hard-working campaigner, approaching any potential voter who would listen, seven days a week. He was elected the fourth time he ran, in 1977, to represent San Francisco's District 5, which included the Haight, Eureka Valley, Noe Valley, Castro, and Diamond Heights neighborhoods. He was the city's first openly gay official.

Two beliefs were central to Milk's philosophy: gay people must come out, and gay people must elect gay representatives.

As Supervisor, Milk battled for gay causes, but also for overlooked groups; including people of color, women, youth, disabled, and the elderly. He worked hard to put together a coalition with other members of the Board of Supervisors.

On November 27, 1978, at age 48, his world stopped when fellow supervisor, Dan White, killed Mayor Moscone (who refused to return White to his supervisory seat) and Milk (who had urged Moscone to give White's position to someone else). The killings tore San Francisco apart and incited gay activists.

There have been many honors since Milk's death: the Presidential Medal of Freedom, having a postage stamp dedicated to him, a naval ship named after him, a park in the Castro District named for him, and having his birthday (May 22) declared Harvey Milk Day.

President Obama presented him the Presidential Medal of Freedom, saying, "Harvey gave us hope, all of us, hope unashamed, hope unafraid."

DIANNE FEINSTEIN

Back to Work

Monday, November 27, 1978 was the first day back to work after three weeks away for Dianne Feinstein. It wasn't going to be an easy day. As president of the San Francisco Board of Supervisors, she ran Board meetings, and Mayor George Moscone had told her he wasn't going to return Dan White to his supervisor position. He asked her to keep White from causing a scene.

At City Hall, Feinstein asked her assistant to find White, and then she began reviewing material for the afternoon's meeting.

She saw White come in and called to him. "Dan, can I talk to you?"

He ignored her, went into Moscone's office, and asked for his position back. Moscone refused. White drew his pistol and shot the mayor. Moscone fell to the floor. White walked to and fired two additional bullets into Moscone's head, killing him.

White left Moscone's office, walked down the hall to Harvey Milk's office, and asked to speak with him. When Milk agreed, White led him across the hall to White's former office and closed the door. Feinstein heard shots.

Jerry Roberts describes her reaction:
She walked down the hall and opened the wrong door, then crossed the hall to White's office and opened that door. Milk was lying face down on the floor. Attempting to find a pulse in his wrist, she put her finger through a bullet hole. She needed help. She tried to contact the police chief but couldn't reach him. Finally he came across the hall and told her the mayor had also been shot and killed.

Feinstein went to her office and composed herself. Her skirt was spotted with Milk's blood and she was shaking. She stood and walked to the balcony outside the Board of Supervisors' chambers and stood next to assistant Peter Nardoza and Police Chief Charles Gain. When she announced the assignations there were shouts and outcries of disbelief.

She returned to her office, gathered her things, and left to comfort the mayor's widow. She was going back to work.

ED LEE

Worth Every Sacrifice

"The community has been waiting for this kind of historic opportunity for many, many decades," Ed Lee said on his first day as mayor. "There have been a lot of sacrifices."

San Francisco's Chinese-American population, which has historically been overlooked and ostracized, has made a lot of sacrifices. But finally Ed Lee, one of them, became mayor.

Lee came from modest beginnings. His parents emigrated from China and settled in Seattle, Washington where he was born in 1952. His father was a cook and restaurant manager, his mother a waitress and seamstress. Lee saw their hard work and sacrifice, and he also saw the prejudice his family sometimes faced.

He washed dishes at a restaurant, studied hard, and graduated from Bowdoin College (Maine) and law school at the University of California. His first law job was with the San Francisco Asian Law Caucus, advocating for affordable housing and tenant rights for immigrants.

Later, he was contentedly working as San Francisco City Administrator when he was chosen by San Francisco's Board of Supervisors to serve as interim mayor, when Gavin Newsom became California's lieutenant governor. As interim His goal was to pull the city together, which he did.

Lee had no plans to run for mayor himself, but a grass-roots campaign engineered in part by San Francisco powerhouses, Rose Pak and Willie Brown, encouraged him to run.

As the votes were tallied on November 8, 2011, Lee was well ahead. He, his family, and a few backers celebrated at a neighborhood restaurant. Then, he reluctantly made his way to a party at the Palace Hotel. He waded through supporters, and took the stage with his wife and daughters. He thanked his family and the volunteers who had helped him so much.

"I'm very humbled," he told the crowd of supporters, "And very tired. But I'm going to work tomorrow, tired or not, because this city is worth every sacrifice."

Then he went home to celebrate quietly with his family.

The "Painted Ladies" at Alamo Square

SAN FRANCISCO WRITERS

Standing in Alamo Square, across from the row of Victorian houses known as the Painted Ladies, it's possible to imagine how San Francisco looked before earthquakes and development. In the late 1800s rows of wooden Victorian houses lined the streets, and City Hall and church steeples pointed to the sky in the distance. Men in dark suits and hats and women in long, black dresses walked the streets and sat on park benches. The city was a sanctuary that inspired emotion and provoked people with a literary bent to write. The fog set the mood, the setting enhanced it, and the open and accepting environment encouraged them to pursue their passions. In their wake they left us their treasures.

MARK TWAIN

Out with the Comet

April 21 is the anniversary of Mark Twain's death. Samuel Clemens (his real name) was 74 when he died in 1910. As a young man he spent time in San Francisco, which was where he became a newspaper reporter, was fired, and where he ultimately found his calling.

Clemens was born in 1835 in the frontier state of Missouri. His father died when he was 12, leaving the family destitute, and a year later Clemens quit school and became a printer's apprentice, setting type and assisting newspaper editors. He lived in Missouri, New York, Pennsylvania, and Ohio; educating himself in public libraries.

He was a steamboat pilot on the Mississippi River, and in 1860 accompanied his brother to Nevada and worked briefly as a gold miner. He hated mining, gave up, and took a job as a reporter at a Virginia City newspaper, using the pen name Mark Twain, a term from his river boating days.

He moved to San Francisco in 1864 and found a job as a reporter for a newspaper called the *Daily Call*. He hated the job, and, after a year-and-a-half, he was fired.

Twain was devastated. He retreated to the Gold Country, lived in a cabin, and drafted an outlandish story about a frog race, but he couldn't finish it. He moved back to San Francisco and spent time "slinking," with no work and little to eat. Then he had a revelation: he should write humorous stories. He finished the piece about the frog, which he called *The Celebrated Jumping Frog of Calaveras County*.

He wrote a series of short stories and books that combined his imagination, writing skills, and characters from his past.

Twain married, had three daughters, and spent the rest of his life writing, travelling, speaking, and promoting his various philosophies. And he always retained a soft spot for San Francisco, where his career began.

In 1909, Twain predicted, "I came in with Halley's Comet in 1835. It is coming again next year and I expect to go out with it."

He was right; he died April 21, 1910 – one day after the comet's closest approach to Earth.

INA COOLBRITH

The Saving Power of Poetry

On top of San Francisco's Russian Hill, on Vallejo Street between Mason and Taylor, is a small park (Ina Coolbrith Park) with wonderful views of the Pyramid Building and Bay Bridge. It's a quiet and secluded spot where tourists and locals can rest, reflect, and read about the San Francisco poet the park is named for.

Ina Donna Coolbrith struggled throughout her life with personal loss, family obligation, and illness. But through dogged persistence she became one of the best-known and most loved poets of her time.

Born in Navoo, Illinois March 10, 1841, her mother named her "Josephina" after her uncle, Joseph Smith (founder of the Morman faith). Her father died of malaria when she was five months old. Her mother remarried, moved the family (including 11-year-old "Ina," as the family called her) by wagon train to California, and supported the family while her new husband invested in failed gold mines. The family relocated to San Francisco, and then Los Angeles.

Ina fell in love with poetry on the way west, reading Shakespeare and Byron, and making up poems during the long, dreary days on the trail. She published her first poem in a Los Angeles newspaper at age 15. Two years later she married Robert Carsely, an ironworker, who abused her, and she lost a baby boy. She divorced, moved to San Francisco, and changed her name to Ina Coolbrith (her mother's maiden name).

San Francisco and poetry became her refuge. She taught school, wrote poems, and developed friendships with writers and poets of the day including Mark Twain, Bret Harte, Charles Stoddard, Joaquin Miller, and Ambrose Bierce. When the all-male Bohemian Club formed in 1872, Ina was named an honorary member.

Ina's responsibilities grew when her sister died and left two children in her care, followed by her ill mother, and Joaquin Miller's daughter. Suddenly, Ina had a lot of mouths to feed. She became head librarian of Oakland's library, where she worked for 18 years. When she was abruptly fired (without cause) she became the Bohemian Club librarian. From her house on Russian Hill, she hosted writing salons and composed poems. Over time, she became a leading West Coast poet, and her work was familiar to a generation of Californians.

Ina never re-married. Men called on her, and friends (including John Muir) tried to play matchmaker. But while she was admired by many men and may have had a tryst or two, in the end her true loves were San Francisco and poetry.

The 1906 earthquake and fire destroyed Ina's house and burned much of her writing. Friends took her in and collected donations to help rebuild her home on Russian Hill. She continued to write poetry and remained a vital part of the San Francisco literary scene for decades. She outlived most of her contemporaries and (despite severe rheumatoid arthritis) continued to write until her death at age 86, February 29, 1928.

There have been many tributes to San Francisco's "Queen of the Meuses." Books have been written about her, a mountain in the Sierras is named for her, and a park on Russian Hill is dedicated to her. But perhaps the utmost recognition was when she was named California's poet laureate (the first in the U.S.) during the 1915 Pan-Pacific Exposition in San Francisco.

On the second day of the exhibition a standing-room-only crowd assembled to see Ina crowned. Poet Edwin Markham described her accomplishments. Senator Phelan introduced her. When the president of the University of California presented her with a laurel crown the audience cheered, waved white handkerchiefs, and threw flowers at her feet.

Ina was typically modest: "For those who are passed away and for my sister women," she told the crowd, "I accept this laurel with deep gratitude and deeper humility."

To San Francisco

Fair on your hills, my City,
Fair as the Queen of old,
Supreme in her seven-hilled splendor-
You, from your Gate of Gold,

Facing the orient sunburst,
Swathed in the sunset gleams,
Throned in an ultimate glory,
City of mists and of dreams!

- Ina Coolbrith

JACK LONDON

Left a Treasure Trove

The odds were stacked against him.

Born in San Francisco in 1876 to an unwed mother, he was named John Griffith Chaney after the itinerant his mother claimed was the father. Unable to care for him, his mother gave him to a friend to raise, and she pursued a husband. She married a man named London, retrieved her son, changed his name, and dragged him along when the family moved around the Bay Area, often living in squalid conditions.

As a boy, London educated himself by reading in libraries (often encouraged by Oakland librarian, Ina Coolbrith). To help support his family he sold newspapers, loaded ice wagons, set pins in a bowling alley, swept saloons, and shoveled coal. At 17, he signed on as a seaman aboard a schooner bound for Hawaii, Japan, and the Bering Sea. On his return, he wrote about his experiences and won first prize in a newspaper contest.

Alaska allured London, and at age 21 he joined the Klondike Gold Rush. He failed to find his fortune and instead became ill, returned to Oakland, and dedicated himself to writing. He struggled, fighting economic hardship and rejection.

He also struggled to find love, impulsively marrying his tutor, Bessie Maddern, and fathering two daughters. Three years later he divorced Bessie and married Charmian Kittredge, who became his soul-mate.

London fell for Sonoma Valley, north of San Francisco, bought a ranch there, and spent his time writing and exploring what he called the Valley of the Moon. He and Charmain designed and built their dream home, which they named Wolf House, but it burned and was never re-built.

London typically wrote 1,000 words a day, which produced more than 40 books and hundreds of short stories and essays.

The illness he developed in Alaska combined with heavy drinking taxed his system and he developed kidney problems in his 30s and died at age 40. He left the world an image of American life at the turn of the 20th century, a wonderful descriptive writing style, and a treasure trove of writing.

DASHIELL HAMMETT

One of the Tough Guys

Samuel Dashiell Hammett lived and wrote in San Francisco, and many of his stories are based there. He became a writer in the city, creating and refining the modern hard-boiled detective story, including his famous novel, *The Maltese Falcon.*

Hammett was born in Maryland in 1894 and grew up in Philadelphia and Baltimore. He became an operative for the Pinkerton Detective Agency when he was 20 and worked in Baltimore, Spokane, and San Francisco. His detective work made him into a tough guy and provided material for his murder mysteries.

Hammett enlisted in the U.S. Army in 1918 and served in World War I. He became ill with influenza, contracted tuberculosis, and recovered in a hospital in Tacoma, Washington, where he fell for a nurse named Josephine Dolan. They married, moved to San Francisco, and raised two daughters.

To make money, Hammett briefly returned to work as a detective, but he was too ill to continue, so he bought a typewriter and wrote whodunits based on his experiences as a detective, selling his work to pulp magazines.

In 1926, Hammett worked briefly as a copywriter for a San Francisco jeweler, but his health no longer allowed him to work full time. The editor of a magazine called *Black Mask* hired him to write mysteries.

As his career took off, his personal life fell apart, and Hammett was forced to live apart from his wife and daughters because of his deteriorating health. At times, he was so weak he was unable to get to the bathroom without help.

But he continued to write, publishing novels and screenplays about crime and love that included snappy dialog and intriguing plots.

Hammett met and fell for Lillian Hellman, a fellow writer, who loved him, fought with him, drank with him, and supported him.

He died in 1961 at age 67, a successful writer, but a broken-down shadow of the tough guy he once was and the tough guys he wrote about.

WILLIAM SAROYAN

Determined to be a Writer

William Saroyan was a San Francisco resident and one of the best-known American authors of the 1930s and 1940s. He wrote fiction, mostly about immigrant life in California during the Depression and World War II.

Saroyan's people were Armenian refugees, who fled to America to escape a massacre by the neighboring Turks. They settled in Fresno, California and toiled to build a new life. His father died when he was four and he and his sister were sent to an orphanage, where they lived four years until their mother could support them.

As a boy, he sold newspapers and did odd jobs to help his family, dropping out of school and teaching himself to read, type, and write.

Determined to be a writer, Saroyan worked doggedly at it, literally starving while awaiting recognition. He moved to Los Angeles, then New York, and finally settled in San Francisco. He worked at odd jobs and supplemented his scarce earnings by gambling.

He wrote short stories but wasn't able to sell them. At that point, most people would give up. Not Saroyan. He wrote to the editor of *Story Magazine* and told him he would write and send a new article each day. He did it, working nearly around the clock, with little other than coffee and cigarettes to keep him going. He received the answer he needed – the editor would publish them!

Eventually, several of Saroyan's stories were combined and published under the title *The Daring Young Man on the Flying Trapeze*. It was a hit.

That led to a successful run during which he wrote screenplays, poetry, and songs, won a Pulitzer Prize for his play, *The Time of Your Life,* and received an Academy Award for best screenplay for the movie, *The Human Comedy*.

He married socialite Carol Marcus, had two children, divorced, remarried, and re-divorced her.

Saroyan died in 1981. He had been a determined writer and a hero to Armenia and Armenian immigrants. Per his instructions, half of his ashes were buried in Fresno; the other half was buried in Armenia.

LAWRENCE FERLINGHETTI

One Fine Day

When he arrived in San Francisco in 1951, Lawrence Ferlinghetti walked up Market Street with a sea bag over his shoulder. He walked a lot that day, and as he wandered he got the impression the people of San Francisco were a little different than average Americans. They seemed to have an "island" mentality, and they were open to new ways of thinking.

That's what he was looking for – a place where he could use poetry to raise America's consciousness. San Francisco, he believed, just might be the place to do it. For the idealistic young poet, that was one fine day!

His early life didn't have a lot of fine days. His father died before he was born and his mother was committed to a psychiatric institution. The boy lived with relatives and in orphanages, then eventually wound up with his aunt in France, and later in New York.

Eventually, the aunt got work as a governess for a wealthy family in New York and Ferlinghetti's luck changed. When the aunt disappeared, the family took the boy in, and his literary education began under the influence of his foster father.

He achieved the rank of Eagle Scout, graduated from college, served in the U. S. Navy during World War II (commanding a patrol boat during the D-Day invasion of France), and was in Nagasaki, Japan a few weeks after the atom bomb was dropped. That experience affected him.

It was an unearthly feeling. The site had been cleaned up – somewhat – or they wouldn't have let us in. I was just off my Navy ship down in southern Kyushu, and we had a day off and went up by train to Nagasaki. It was pretty horrible to see. And that was just a toy bomb compared to the ones that are available today.

— Lawrence Ferlinghetti

He set out to make the world a more peaceful and equitable place.

As an aspiring writer in Paris, Ferlinghetti was influenced by American writers T.S. Eliot and Ezra Pound, and he taught himself some of their techniques.

Eventually, he became convinced that he was imitating them, not developing a unique voice, and he found a different prototype in Kenneth Rexroth, a poet, author, and translator.

In San Francisco, Ferlinghetti supported himself by teaching, freelance writing, and translating French poetry. He and Rexroth wrote and read poetry, often at the Cellar, a North Beach jazz nightclub.

In 1953, Ferlinghetti and Peter Martin founded a bookstore and publishing house in North Beach, which they named *City Lights*. They published books by local poets and authors, including the controversial book "Howl," by Allen Ginsberg.

Ferlinghetti has become part of San Francisco's legend; writing poetry, creating art, and helping young poets publish their works.

During his time in San Francisco, Ferlinghetti has had many fine days.

He has been given numerous awards and honors for his art and poetry, including the Robert Frost Memorial Medal, the Author's Guild Lifetime Achievement Award, and being named San Francisco's first poet laureate.

He is humble, and those awards have not distracted him from his attempts to make the world a better place.

"One Fine Day," one of Ferlinghetti's most moving poems, describes his view of everyday life. Perhaps it is his way of saying that despite our troubles we can all find an inner peace.

One Fine Day

By Lawrence Ferlinghetti

One grand boulevard with trees
with one grand café in sun
with strong black coffee in very small cups.

One not necessarily very beautiful
man or woman who loves you.
One fine day.

The Changing Light

By Lawrence Ferlinghetti

The changing light at San Francisco
is none of your East Coast light
none of your
pearly light of Paris
The light of San Francisco
is a sea light
an island light
And the light of fog
blanketing the hills
drifting in at night
through the Golden Gate
to lie on the city at dawn
And then the halcyon late mornings
after the fog burns off
and the sun paints white houses
with the sea light of Greece
with sharp clean shadows
making the town look like
it had just been painted
But the wind comes up at four o'clock
sweeping the hills
And then the veil of light of early evening
And then another scrim
when the new night fog
floats in
And in that vale of light
the city drifts
anchorless upon the ocean

HERB CAEN

Part of San Francisco's Everyday Life

Herb Caen was part of everyday life in San Francisco for more than 60 years. He wrote a column for the *San Francisco Chronicle* that included local goings-on, insider gossip, and social and political happenings. He called it "a continuous love letter to San Francisco," and it was the first thing many people in San Francisco read each morning.

His first column appeared July 5, 1938, and Caen continued to write it six days a week until 1991, when he cut back to five, and later to three days.

"I can't find a way out," he told the *New York Times*, "There are too many bills and ex-wives and a kid in school, things that chew up the income. I never intended this to be permanent, but it looks like it's going to be."

Caen wrote in the morning, adjourned to lunch (usually with colleagues, and often with drinks). In the evenings he attended social events and took the pulse of the city he called "Baghdad by the Bay." He wrote with two fingers on a manual typewriter, telling who was doing what, passing on witticisms, and offering opinions.

"Don't call it Frisco," he told his readers, repeating Emperor Norton's command. He coined the term "Beatnik" and called his favorite drink, vodka, "vitamin V." He sometimes attributed observations to a mysterious "Strange de Jim," who had no other identity and who many suspected was Caen's alter-ego.

He wrote to the end, from lung cancer, in 1997, at 80. Why didn't he quit sooner? "Because my name wouldn't be in the paper and I wouldn't know if I was dead or alive," he told the *New York Times*.

The city that loved Caen held a candlelight parade after his death in February of 1997. Thousands of San Franciscans participated, marching down Market Street carrying candles and reminiscing, with little in common except that they were all grateful to Herb for entertaining them for so long.

CARL NOLTE

News Doesn't Happen in the Office

Carl Nolte has been around San Francisco for more than 80 years. He is a fourth-generation San Franciscan, former soldier, avid sailor, adventurer, and hiker. Reared in the City's Potrero Hill neighborhood, he has many happy memories of his childhood in a city very different than it is today.

"It was a great place to grow up," he has written. "There were steam trains, billy goats, grass bombs, Russians with long white beards, lumber yards, fleabag movies, the famous summer days when the San Francisco Fire Department set the whole hill on fire, kite flying contests, cliffs, unpaved streets, even sailing rafts on flooded ponds on the south side of the hill. They had anti-aircraft guns in the park, and the Bay was full of ships. Jeez, you shoulda been there."

Nolte was drafted and spent two years in the U.S. Army and three in the reserves, including a year in Korea, after the war. He was a soldier in the Cold War, and was a war correspondent in the Gulf War and the 2003 invasion of Iraq. During the second Iraq war, he was imbedded inside a Bradley fighting vehicle as part of his old unit – the U.S. Army's Charlie Company, Third Battalion, Seventh Regiment.

"That one wasn't too easy," he wrote, "I was 69 at the time."

Nolte has been in the news reporting business all his adult life. His first day at the *San Francisco Chronicle* was in June, 1961, "a lifetime ago." Hired to work on the copy desk, edit stories, and write headlines, he sat there, waiting for an assignment, apprehensive, like a kid on the first day of school.

He has held several positions during his time at the *Chronicle;* including war correspondent, news reporter, copy editor, and assistant city editor. He is currently a reporter and columnist and writes the "Native Son" column for the Sunday paper.

He prefers being a reporter to an editor. For one thing, he says, it's your fault if you're an editor, and the other thing is you have to stay in the headquarters, and "news doesn't happen in the office."

Tribute to the Summer of Love
at The Conservatory of Flowers

THE SUMMER OF LOVE

The summer of 1967 was a trying time for San Francisco. The Vietnam War, social unrest, and struggles between the hippies pouring in and the police trying to restrain them created an atmosphere of turmoil and strife. There were problems that summer including violence, drug overdoses, and illnesses but it was also a time of invention and creativity. People were trying new things; different ways of thinking, living, and being. And they were creating new and exciting music.

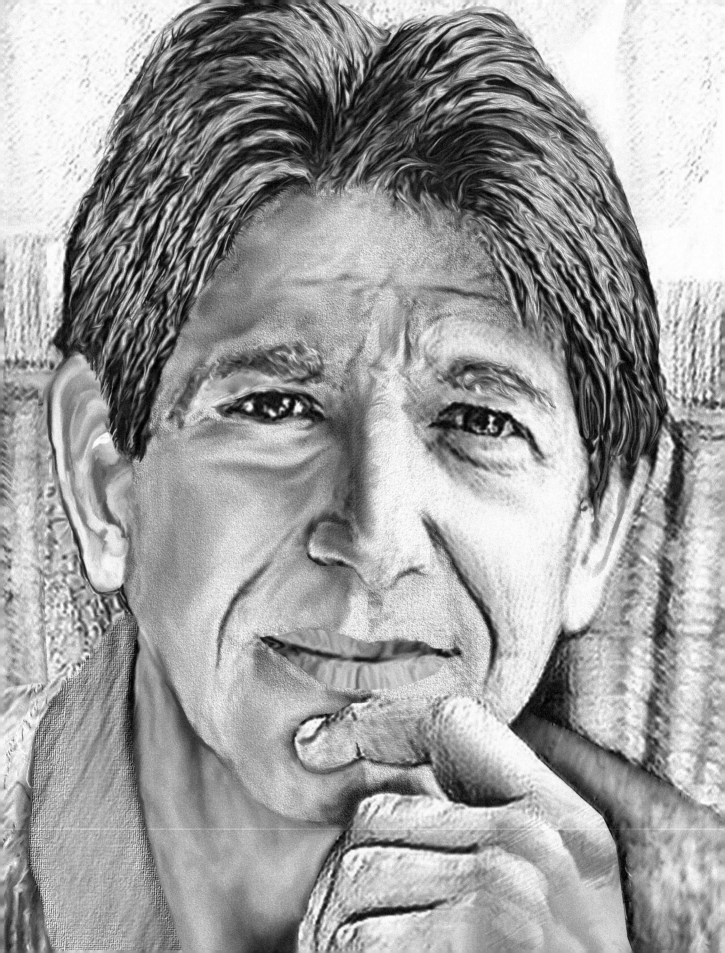

PETER COYOTE

Love, Power, and Wisdom

Peter Coyote considered the Summer of Love an experiment during a period of optimism. It turned into a bit of a mess, and while it didn't solve the world's political problems, it did accomplish some goals. In its wake are forces that continue to influence our lives; including love, power, and wisdom.

Born in Manhattan as Robert Peter Cohon, Coyote had a privileged but unusual childhood. His father was a successful businessman who was hard on his son; his mother was often depressed.

He got involved in politics and acting, was an activist in college, and moved to San Francisco to study creative writing. He joined the San Francisco Mime Troupe, met and befriended Bill Graham, and cofounded a group called the Diggers, who gathered leftover food, fed the hippies who streamed to the city in 1967, opened free health clinics, found places for runaways to sleep, and opened a free store.

He changed his name (based on an experience with coyotes during a peyote ceremony), turned to meditation and communal living, studied Buddhism, served on the California Arts Council, and launched an acting career. Today, he is known for appearing in movies and narrating documentaries.

Asked whether the Diggers accomplished their goals during the Summer of Love, Coyote says they lost the political battles and didn't end war, capitalism, racism, or imperialism. "But," he insists, "If you look at the cultural front, we changed everything."

Today he feels good. He is a successful author, father, and actor and he says it is a heady experience to do something you love and get paid for it.

He looks back on his life and sees three main influences: love, power, and wisdom.

"Love without power is flaccid," he believes, "And power without love is cruel." He believes there is a third choice. "And that is wisdom. I made the decision to spend the rest of my life listening to it and, to the best of my abilities, speaking to it."

That's what he learned during the Summer of Love, and it's what drives him today.

Bill Graham

Laughter, Love, and Music

He helped create music that brought people to San Francisco during the Summer of Love and he became one of rock and roll's most influential figures. Despite a difficult start, he led a life filled with laughter, love, and music.

Bill Graham's birth name was Wolfgang Grajonca; he was born in Berlin in 1931 to Russian Jewish emigrants. His father died when he was two days old. At eight, he and his sister, Tolla, were sent to an orphanage in Paris, to save them from Nazi persecution. When the Nazis overran Paris, the Red Cross led him and 63 other children to Portugal, much of the way on foot. Tolla didn't survive.

At Lisbon, he was put on a refugee ship for New York, where he was placed in an orphanage until adopted by foster parents. No one could pronounce his name, so he took another, from a phone book.

Bill Graham, as he now called himself, served in the U.S. Army during the Korean War and worked as a taxi driver in New York, a waiter in the Catskills, and then came to San Francisco to visit his sister. He fell for the city, moved there, took an office job, and worked on the side booking appearances for the San Francisco Mime Troupe.

When the Troupe ran into legal trouble, Graham organized a concert to raise funds for them. He found he liked working with bands and bringing music to people.

He produced concerts full-time, doing it all: distributing posters, collecting tickets at the door, even cleaning the bathrooms.

Graham helped launch the careers of rock and roll bands; including the Grateful Dead, Jefferson Airplane, Jimi Hendrix, Santana, Led Zeppelin, the Rolling Stones, and many others. He was one of the first to produce concerts for humanitarian causes.

He was 60 when his helicopter crashed while flying home from a concert in bad weather. All three people on board died. A memorial in Golden Gate Park was attended by 300,000 people, with music by bands he had helped start. It was a fitting tribute to the man who had overcome hardship, brought people together, and helped a new generation experience laughter, love, and music.

JANIS JOPLIN

Do One Thing Well

In the middle of her wistful song, *Cry Baby*, Janis Joplin's voice softens and she implores listeners to find something to do with their life. "You only gotta do one thing well," she says, "To make it in this world." That epitomizes her life, which was a search for acceptance, success, and for one thing she could do well.

Eventually, she did find her "thing," and for a while she was the brightest star in rock-and-roll.

Growing up in Port Arthur, Texas, Joplin was popular through the ninth grade, but was then shunned by her classmates because she was different. That affected her.

Bored and restless, she quit college and moved to San Francisco, where she hung out with Beatniks and sang in clubs. In time, she joined the hippy revolution, experimented with drugs, and had numerous short-term affairs.

Strung out on alcohol and drugs, she returned to Texas, vowing to pursue a "normal" lifestyle. It didn't last and she moved back to San Francisco. This time she put her whole self into singing, airing her emotions through music.

Her break came in June, 1967, when she performed with Big Brother and the Holding Company at the Monterrey Pop Festival. She rocked the audience and earned good reviews from music critics.

She toured, cut an album (*Cheap Thrills*), and appeared on television. She was a star, albeit a strange one, with a screeching voice, outlandish behavior, and foul language.

In 1970, she went back to Texas for her 10-year high school reunion and another attempt at acceptance. It was a disaster. She embarrassed her family, her classmates, and herself, and she went back to California discouraged.

She began using drugs again, and on October 4, 1970, in Los Angeles she went to her motel room shot up heroin, and died. She was 27.

Her life was filled with ups-and-downs, but the person who once described herself as "this chick who was good at this one thing, man" managed to find something she could do well, and she had done it.

JERRY GARCIA

I Play for My Life

Jerry Garcia used to tell a story about an incident at a concert the Grateful Dead played in San Francisco's Fillmore Auditorium. Before the concert someone brought in a birthday cake, and Garcia scooped up and ate a fingerfull of frosting. Just then, the guy who brought the cake warned that the frosting was laced with LSD. "Oh no," thought Garcia, "Now I'm going to be tripping the whole concert."

He did, hallucinating that the audience was filled with members of the mafia, who were going to kill him. "What can I do?" he asked himself. "I know … I'll play for my life. So I did, and they let me live. Ever since, when I forget what I'm doing, or why I'm doing it, I play for my life."

Garcia played for his life for more than 30 years, almost exclusively with the Grateful Dead. He was an integral part of the Summer of Love, and a popular figure in contemporary San Francisco.

Garcia learned to play the banjo and acoustic guitar as a boy. After a brief stint in the Army, he moved to Palo Alto, played with a jug band and then the Warlocks, who became the Grateful Dead. Their first album was released in 1967 during the Summer of Love. They played at the Human Be-In, Monterrey Pop Festival, and San Francisco's Avalon Ballroom and Fillmore Auditorium. Garcia met promoter Bill Graham, who called Garcia "Big Papa Bear."

The Grateful Dead played concerts and recorded music for the next three decades and had a loyal following called "Deadheads" who attended their concerts and even followed them around the country. Garcia loved it all. "Hell yes," he said, "I get to play music, and I get paid for it. That's incredible! I mean, I met Bob Dylan, man!"

Garcia was overweight most of his adult life, and he smoked cigarettes and used drugs. In 1995, five days after his 53rd birthday, he passed away in his sleep in a northern California rehab center. He had played his last gig, sung his last song. San Francisco and the rest of the world had lost its big papa bear – the man who had played for his life.

GRACE SLICK

One Thing at a Time

She has said she's not a good multitasker and thinks doing one thing at a time is best: one man, one child, one career.

That approach has worked for her, and Grace Slick has had a rewarding life as a musician, song writer, artist, and mother, and she has few regrets. And, for one special summer in 1967, she spearheaded a social movement in San Francisco as the unofficial queen of the "Summer of Love."

Grace Wing grew up in a middle-class family, attended college, and moved to San Francisco. She worked as a model for San Francisco's legendary I. Magnin department store, married Jerry Slick (an aspiring filmmaker), and wrote songs for him.

In the spring of 1965, she met a band called the *Jefferson Airplane*. She was taken with their music, and she and Jerry started a similar band called the *Great Society*.

The lead singer for *Jefferson Airplane* quit, so Slick stepped in. They played a blend of jazz, folk, rock and blues, which Slick referred to as "electric freak stuff."

The band bought a Victorian mansion near Golden Gate Park where they practiced and partied, often with other local musicians including Jerry Garcia and Janis Joplin. Their music took off, and their album, *Surrealistic Pillow,* was a top-seller.

For Slick, the Summer of Love was an omen. She believes music, poetry, and art are cues about who we want to be and how we want to get there, and she sees the Summer of Love as a reminder of our possibilities and the future we're trying to build.

She left rock & roll in her 40's because she didn't want to outlive her usefulness. She put it bluntly, saying "prancing around on a stage is not the entire purpose of my life." She settled in a San Francisco cottage and concentrated on art, painting images of musicians and people she knew.

Slick has been successful – she beat addiction, overcame loneliness, and achieved happiness and peace. "I did pretty much most of the stuff I had in mind," she has said, "One thing at a time."

CARLOS SANTANA

Helping the World Heal

For Carlos Santana, the Summer of Love was the beginning of a period of peace and acceptance. The music played that summer, he believed, promoted understanding and love, and he wanted to be part of helping the world heal. But first, he needed to set himself right.

Born in 1947 in a small coastal Mexican village, Santana was raised in a large and dysfunctional family. His father was gone a lot, playing violin in mariachi bands.

When his family moved to Tijuana, he played music for money on the streets and in strip clubs. His family moved to San Francisco, but he left them, went back to Tijuana, and resumed his strip club job. He eventually joined his family and attended high school in San Francisco, but he had little interest other than music.

During the Summer of Love, Santana moved in with friends and busked for coins. He hung out at the Fillmore Auditorium, where Bill Graham let him fill in for musicians who didn't show or were too stoned to perform.

He formed the Santana Blues Band, and played at the Human Be-In, Monterrey Pop Festival, and opened for bands like Chicago and Steppenwolf. They signed with Columbia Records and recorded a successful album. When they played at Woodstock, people really began to notice them.

In 1972, he met Deborah, for whom he immediately fell. They married, raised three children, and became followers of the guru, Sri Chinmoy. He signed Bill Graham as his manager, and they worked well together, cut albums, and toured.

His relationship with Columbia Records ended in 1990, the same year Graham died. It was a lot to deal with. Santana went to therapy, learned to cope with his issues, and added spirituality and meditation to his life.

He continued to write and record music and in 1999 produced an album called *Supernatural* that was a massive success, winning nine Grammy Awards. "Music is the vehicle for the magic of healing," he said as he accepted the award for album of the year.

It was the pinnacle of a long and successful career – a lifetime of helping the world heal.

Willie Mays statue in front of Oracle Park

SAN FRANCISCO AT PLAY

San Francisco has had a history of great sports teams. Most people are familiar with the Super Bowl championships of the 49ers, the World Series victories of the Giants, and the NBA champion Golden State Warriors. Each of those teams featured individuals with leadership skills, talent, and perseverance. There has also been a history of dominant athletes in individual sports; like boxing, golf, and tennis. The stories behind them are as interesting as the accomplishments they achieved.

Joe DiMaggio

The End of the Streak

Joe DiMaggio grew up in San Francisco's North Beach neighborhood near Fisherman's Wharf, where his father was a fisherman. As a young man, Joe played baseball for the minor league San Francisco Seals in the now-defunct Seals Stadium. In 1936 he was scouted and signed by the New York Yankees.

"Joltin' Joe" DiMaggio became one of the most successful baseball players of all times, and one of the most well-known people of his era. Today, he is often remembered for being married to Marilyn Monroe – and for "the streak."

It started May 15, 1941. DiMaggio hit safely that night and at least once in each of the next 55 games.

The climax took place July 17, 1941. The game in Cleveland that night between the Yankees and Cleveland Indians had the potential to extend the streak, and each of DiMaggio's at-bats was an event. The whole stadium paid attention when he came to the plate.

Some Cleveland fans weren't sure whether to hope he got a hit (and kept his streak going) or made an out (to help their team). Either way, they were witnessing history.

DiMaggio went hitless his first three times at-bat: a ground ball out to the infield, a walk, and a grounder to third base that turned into an out.

He had one more chance in the eighth inning, when he came to bat with the bases loaded. On the fourth pitch DiMaggio hit a feeble ground ball to the shortstop, who grabbed it, threw it to the second baseman, who relayed it to first for a double play. The Yankees won the ball game (the final score was 4-3), but the streak was over.

After the game, DiMaggio wrestled with two emotions: happiness his team had won, (the Yankees' success was always more important to him than his individual achievement), and sadness he had not had a better day.

After the game he waited for the crowd to thin and then left the stadium with Phil Rizzuto, his teammate and friend. They walked to their hotel discussing the game. Then DiMaggio went to dinner, by himself. It had been another day in a long and successful career, and he had a lot to be grateful for. But at that moment, above all else, he was thankful to have reached the end of the streak.

WILLIE MAYS

Kept His Cool

Willie Mays was one of the best baseball players of all times. He played 21 seasons with the Giants (New York and San Francisco), and his career statistics were astonishing! But his introduction to San Francisco was harsh.

The Giants announced plans to move to San Francisco in 1958, and Mays and his wife, Marghuerite, decided to buy a house and move from New York. Marghuerite arrived in San Francisco first and found a house she liked in an upscale neighborhood. She met with the owner, a man named Walter Gnesdiloff, agreed on a price, and put down a deposit.

When word spread that the owner was talking to the Mays' the neighbors called to complain. Some worried the value of their homes would go down if a black family moved in; others simply didn't want a black family living in their neighborhood.

The next day Willie arrived, and he and Marghuerite went to pay the balance. When they arrived, the owner told them the house was no longer for sale.

The front page of the *San Francisco Chronicle* told the story:

"Willie Mays is Denied House in S.F. – Race Issue."

Mays said little. "I've never been through this kind of stuff and I'm not even mad about it now," he told reporters. "I'd sure like to live in San Francisco, but I didn't want to make an issue about it."

Mayor George Christopher got involved and met with civil rights leader, Edward Howden, to convince the objecting neighbors that their property values would go up, not down, with the most famous baseball player in the world living in their midst. It worked. The next day Gnesdiloff changed his mind: he would sell to the Mays'.

Mays kept his cool throughout the incident, refusing to give in to prejudice and hate. He had a personal philosophy that helps understand why: "I was very fortunate to play sports," he once said. "All the anger in me went out. I had to do what I had to do. If you stay angry all the time, then you really don't have a good life."

JOE MONTANA

Mr. Big Game

All NFL quarterbacks are great athletes, and all have survived intense competition to reach their level. With little difference in size or strength, less tangible attributes separate those who excel from those who don't. Chief among those qualities is the ability to perform in significant situations. In that regard, Joe Montana stood out as one of the best "big game" quarterbacks of all times.

Montana was a talented athlete in high school and college, where he led Notre Dame to a comeback Cotton Bowl win and a national championship. Drafted by the 49ers, he played under legendary coach Bill Walsh and guided the team to three Super Bowl victories.

Montana had many big games, but perhaps his greatest was Super Bowl XXIII, January 22, 1989, in Miami's Joe Robbie Stadium, against the Cincinnati Bengals.

It was a close contest all the way, and the Bengals led 16-13, with just 3:20 remaining. The 49ers had the ball at their own 8-yard line. Montana ran onto the field and into the huddle. The 49ers started with three completed passes, then two running plays, and another pass. Now they were past mid-field. Another completed pass put the ball at Cincinnati's 35, but an incomplete pass and a penalty put them out of field goal range … and almost out of time.

Montana threw a slant-in pass to Jerry Rice, who zigged and zagged through defenders to the Bengal's 18. The 49ers were back in field goal range, but Mr. Big Game wasn't thinking about a field goal – he wanted a touchdown.

He passed to Roger Craig, who ran to the 10-yard line, and then called time-out. Thirty-nine seconds left. On the next play Montana faded back, looked at Craig, saw he was covered, and threw a perfect chest-high spiral in the end zone to John Taylor. The 49ers jumped on each other and the stadium went nuts. They held on to win – an improbable comeback and an amazing victory!

It was a satisfying win for Montana and his teammates, and a nice send-off for Bill Walsh, who retired as head coach. NFL commissioner, Pete Rozelle, called it "the finest of our 23 Super Bowls." It was a thrilling game, won by a team with guts, led by Mr. Big Game.

JOHNNY MILLER

Golfing Nirvana

Achieving the pinnacle of your profession is something many of us dream of, but few realize. But Johnny Miller did it. He won 25 PGA tournaments, was named to the World Golf Hall of Fame, and has had a satisfying career as a television golf analyst. He has had success besides golfing, too, having written a book about golf, a column for *Golf Digest*, and he's a part-owner and designer of world-class golf courses.

Born and raised in San Francisco, Miller learned golf from his father. As a Boy Scout, he learned to leave his campsite better than he found it, a lesson he has applied to his life. He won his first golf title at 16, and was a golf star at BYU. He joined the PGA Tour in 1969, at age 22, and won his first tour event in 1971.

For Miller, the early 1970s were as good as it gets. Between 1973 and 1976, he was one of the most accurate iron players of all time and a dominant force in golf. In 1973, he played one of the most remarkable rounds in major championship history, shooting a final day round of 63, which was the lowest ever in a U.S. Open.

Over the next two years, he won 12 tournaments and experienced times when his game was almost magic, finding he "could knock down the pin from anywhere."

But Miller ran into a slump in the late 1970s. After re-shaping his body during a summer of hard physical labor, he found he could no longer swing gold clubs the same. He got the "yips" (missed easy putts) and didn't have the drive to win. But he remained steady, never showed bitterness, and never refused an interview.

He battled back, won a few tournaments, and accepted a position as a television golf analyst. It's been a good second career.

Miller would likely say he has had a satisfying life. He reached the top of his profession and achieved greatness. And he believes the true test in life is not what you accomplish, but what you overcome.

"Sometimes," he said, "I think that when we get up in heaven, God's going to let everyone be 28, and there's going to be this great tournament."

That would be his golfing nirvana.

ALICE MARBLE

A Story for the Ages

Alice Marble was a tomboy in 1920s San Francisco with a great interest in baseball. She attended local minor league San Francisco Seals games, arriving early to shag flies for Lefty O'Doul and Joe DiMaggio. Her brother didn't like his sister "acting like a boy" so he gave her a racquet and told her to play tennis.

She did, and over time she became a champion tennis player; touring the U.S., Canada, and Europe, winning most of the time.

After collapsing from tuberculosis during a tennis match, Marble made a remarkable comeback, from near death to become the best female tennis player in the world. She gave inspirational talks, conducted tennis clinics, had her own line of women's tennis clothing, and hung out with such notables as Clark Gable, Charlie Chaplin, and Randolph Hearst.

During World War II, Marble co-chaired a physical-fitness program, conducted tennis clinics for soldiers, and performed as a singer at U.S.O. clubs. She married a pilot named Joe Crowley, who was killed on Christmas Eve in 1944. After his death she fell apart, recovered, and was recruited by the U.S. Army and trained as a spy. She was asked to renew contact with a former lover named Hans (a Nazi sympathizer) in Switzerland, and to obtain information from him.

She went to Europe and played in tennis matches to attract Hans. It worked. She dated him and discovered he kept a key to a safe with stolen valuables and names of the Nazis who had stolen them.

She photographed the information and was about to turn it over to U.S. authorities when she discovered her contact was a double-agent. As she fled from him he shot her in the back, took the photographs, and turned them over to the Russians.

Badly wounded, Marble spent months recovering in a hospital. She was able to recall some of the names and information, which helped prosecute Nazi officers.

Marble spent the rest of her life mentoring female tennis players (including Billy Jean King), and supporting desegregation of the sport. In 1964, she was inducted into the International Tennis Hall of Fame. She was an innovator, champion, and hero, and her story is one for the ages.

JIM CORBETT

Gentleman Jim

Professional boxing is in decline these days, with occasional matches sparsely followed on cable or pay-per-view. But, a century ago, prize-fighting was widely popular. Championship bouts drew huge crowds and were followed by millions of fans. That was due, in part, to a San Franciscan known as "Gentleman Jim" Corbett.

Born in 1866 to Irish immigrants, Corbett grew up in a middle-class family in post-Gold Rush San Francisco. He graduated from Sacred Heart High School, attended college, and worked in a local bank.

He learned to box at the Olympic Club, and in his first pro fight, at age 18, he displayed a new and innovative style that included defensive maneuvers, side-stepping, circling and gliding, and sharp, quick punches – all very different from traditional flat-footed slugging.

Corbett gained recognition when he fought Peter Jackson, a well-respected boxer from Australia. It went 61 rounds and ended in a draw. The reigning champion, John L. Sullivan, agreed to fight Corbett in New Orleans in September, 1892. It was the first heavyweight championship fight under the Marquess of Queensbury Rules, which required gloves and breaks between rounds. Corbett boxed circles around Sullivan; dancing, jabbing, and counter-punching. He broke Sullivan's nose in the fifth round and knocked him out in in the 21st round. The world had a new champion and new style of boxing.

Corbett seldom defended his title, instead appearing on stage and in plays and movies. He was handsome, well-dressed, and used proper grammar, and he was popular with men, who identified with him, and women, who liked his looks and style. He lost his title to Bob Fitzsimmons in 1897, and retired from boxing in 1903. Errol Flynn later portrayed him in a movie titled *Gentleman Jim*.

Few of us have the opportunity to affect a profession, but Corbett did. He changed boxing from brutal to genteel, and in the process he earned a reputation that matched his nickname – Gentleman Jim.

San Francisco's Castro District

In Their Own Way

There is an unconventional facet of San Francisco, populated by people who don't think and act like everyone else. Many are compassionate individuals: artists, educators, or humanitarians with traits in common: they are leaders dedicated to their cause, and they adamantly pursue their passion. Behind, they leave traces of creativity and kindness.

CLEVE JONES

The Movement

The movement defined his purpose, gave him hope, and saved his life. Fighting for gay rights gave him a reason to get out of bed each morning and carry on through prejudice, illness, and loss.

Cleve Jones grew up in a household where his father, a psychologist, did the best he could. But Jones couldn't confide in him when he realized he was gay, so he kept it secret and plotted suicide if it was discovered.

As a teenager, Jones saw an article about gay liberation in *Life* magazine, including photos of young gay men in San Francisco marching with their fists in the air, coming "out of the closets and into the streets."

That inspired Jones, and he moved to San Francisco, joined the gay rights movement, and became an intern for Harvey Milk. He was crushed by Milk's assassination, but struggled through, fighting for visibility and equal rights.

Then the AIDS epidemic struck the gay community, including Jones, and he watched as his friends died. He made new friends, who also died. He helped establish the San Francisco AIDS Foundation to provide HIV education, advocacy, prevention, and care.

As friends continued to die, Jones and fellow activists posted names of AIDS victims on a downtown San Francisco building, which inspired them to turn the tribute into the NAMES Project AIDS Memorial Quilt. Jones successfully campaigned against California's Proposition 8, which would have banned same-sex marriage.

Today, he continues to fight for the movement – pursuing equal rights for everyone.

Despite a difficult life and many losses, Jones is happy – filled with love, life, and the ability to see the good in things. His face reflects hardships, but he isn't bitter, and he says he did what he wanted and has much to look forward to. He asks others to do what they can to reach out to others, find common ground, and help the movement.

CAROL DODA

A Good Time

Carol Doda and the Condor Club were part of the San Francisco nightclub scene for more than two decades. Sailors, businessmen, and politicians made their way to the club on Broadway Street to see the first public topless dancer. Local newspapers and TV stations covered her act, and her performance was the talk of the town. She knew how to show people a good time.

Doda grew up in San Francisco, dropped out of school at 14, took voice lessons, and worked as a cocktail waitress and lounge entertainer. She performed her first topless dance at 19, wearing a "monokini" swimsuit designed by fashion icon Rudi Gernreich.

Her act gained publicity and was a popular tourist destination. She made up to 12 appearances per night, pushing the edges to keep customers coming. Silicon injections increased her breasts from 34B to 44DD and she performed nude for a while until a law prohibited it. She was arrested once, for indecency, but was acquitted.

In her act, a spotlight lit up a white baby grand piano that was slowly lowered from the ceiling of the club. Doda stood atop the piano, topless, proudly displaying her 44-inch bust. She danced and swiveled through a few songs, and then the piano rose back to the ceiling with Doda waving and blowing kisses to the audience.

Doda quit dancing topless in 1985, but she remained part of the San Francisco scene for another two decades. She never married, but had two children, who were not close to her.

After the Condor Club, Doda started a band called "Carol Doda and the Lucky Stiffs," and she was still dancing in 2009 in North Beach clubs, fully-clothed. She once said the only way she would stop performing is "when I can't walk any more, honey." She died November 9, 2015.

Asked about her act, Doda said, "It was never just about being topless anyway. I always just wanted to give people a good time."

DON NOVELLO

Father Guido Sarducci

Don Novello didn't start out as a comedian. He studied business in college, worked as an advertising copywriter, and appeared headed for a business career. But his life changed when he came up with the idea of doing comedy to lighten the mood of the 1970s, which were tainted by Watergate and Vietnam.

Novello created a character, loosely based on Jesuit priests he met while studying in Rome, and he included a black robe, white collar, mustache, cigarette, tinted eyeglasses, and Italian accent.

In 1972, he appeared as Father Guido Sarducci on the *Chicken Little Comedy Show* for a San Francisco TV station. Comic David Steinberg was watching and he liked the act. He hired Novello as a TV writer and introduced him to Tommy and Dick Smothers, who added him to *The Smothers Brothers' Show*.

Lorne Michaels, producer of *Saturday Night Live*, heard about Novello, hired him as a writer, and also added his Father Guido Sarducci character to the show – a record thirty-one times.

Novello has had a full career as an actor, writer, director, comedian, and producer. He has written books and plays and performed in movies, on television, and on stage.

Some of his observations are classics; including his riff on becoming a saint.

"To be made a saint in-a the Catholic Church, you have to have-a four miracles. That's-a the rule, you know. It's-a always been that-a four miracles, and-a to prove it.

Well, this-a Mother Seton-now they could only prove-a three miracles. But the Pope-he just waived the fourth one. He just waived it! And do you know why? It's-a because she was American. It's all-a politics.

We got-a some Italian-a people, they got-a forty, fifty, sixty miracles to their name. They can't-a get in just cause they say there's already too many Italian saints, and this-a woman she comes along with-a three lousy miracles. I understand that-a two of them was-a card tricks."

Don Novello is a well-known character in the Bay Area, where he has performed at numerous charity appearances. He has found a welcoming home, fame, and a sense of purpose in the City by the Bay.

DON HERRON

Shadowing Dashiell Hammett

Don Herron waits for his Dashiell Hammett tour group on a San Francisco street corner. The years and the San Francisco fog have drained some of the color from him, and his hair and beard are turning gray. His face and hands have also taken on a gray tint. His attire is subdued – a well-worn tan fedora, open tan trench coat, black shirt and tie, tan slacks, and brown shoes. He could fit in on the streets of San Francisco in the 1920s.

Herron came to San Francisco in 1974, and three years later he recognized the value of a Dashiell Hammett tour so he designed it, trademarked it, and began operating it for a living. Since then, he has led it hundreds of times, and it's now the longest-running literary tour in the nation.

He is a wealth of knowledge about Dashiell Hammett, San Francisco, and 20th-century American literature. He talks nearly non-stop during the four-hour tour, relating stories about the neighborhood, Dashiell Hammett, and Sam Spade.

The tour begins at the Samuels' clock in front of the Flood Building, on San Francisco's Market Street. Herron points out John's Grill (where Hammett dined), and locations in Hammett's books; including the Geary Theater, the Palace Hotel, the Stockton Tunnel, and Burritt Street, where (in *The Maltese Falcon*) Brigid O'Shaughnessy shot Miles Archer. He describes where Hammett slept, where he wrote, and where his characters lived and died.

The final stop is 891 Post Street, the apartment building where Hammett lived while writing *The Maltese Falcon*. Herron turns to face the group and points his thumbs back at the building while telling the story.

Today, Don lives in two distinct worlds: the high-tech, instant communication world of the 21st century, and the hard-boiled, shadowy world of Dashiell Hammett's roaring '20s. He seems to enjoy both.

When he isn't giving the tour or lecturing to clubs, Don manages a website and blog on Dashiell Hammett and other mystery writers. He has figured out how to spend this part of his life – doing something he loves, and making a living doing it.

LEE ROBERSON

They Will Always Be His Kids

Lee Roberson saw a lot of kids go through Telegraph Hill Neighborhood Center (Tel-Hi) and he saw a lot of change in nearly 20 years there, but one thing always stayed the same: "To be successful," he often said, "You have to put your heart and soul into the job."

He did put his heart and soul into helping the Tel-Hi kids, and the hundreds of lives he touched were better because of it. Most of the kids lived in public housing and many belonged to single-parent families. Some of their friends and relatives wound up in trouble, but few of Lee's kids did.

Roberson was youth director for Tel-Hi from 1970 through 1989. His goal was to gain the kids' trust. "I told them if you respect me, I will respect you," he said. They did, and they generally followed his advice.

He saw the need to keep the kids busy with year-round recreational activities, so he started and ran basketball programs. Over time, he added other recreational activities; including volleyball, chess, ping pong, track, baseball, weightlifting, parade drill teams, and classes in dance, art, and photography – all designed to provide positive outlet for their creativity and energy.

There was an instance when basketballs were disappearing and he confronted the kids. "Those balls aren't mine," he told them. "They're yours. And when they're gone, there won't be any more." There weren't any more missing basketballs after that.

His reward for his two decades at Tel-Hi was watching the kids grow up, graduate from school, and become successful adults.

Roberson stayed in touch with many of the kids, helping them through problems, or just being there for them. Watching them grow and staying in touch with them meant a lot to him, because they will always be his kids.

BOB DAMIR

A Very Special Favor

San Francisco attorney Bob Damir faced a dilemma when his friend, William Saroyan, died in 1981. Saroyan, a well-known mid-20th century author, had requested that half of his ashes be buried in Armenia, his ancestor's homeland, and Damir was asked to help deliver them. That was a very special favor, since it would mean travelling to the U.S.S.R., which had a tense relationship with the U.S.

He decided he needed to do this for his friend, so he reluctantly told his family, arranged time away from his office, and had a travel agent organize the trip.

He flew (with Saroyan's ashes in an urn) from San Francisco to Toronto, and then to Montreal. The next morning he boarded a crowded, uncomfortable Russian airplane to Moscow. Going through customs in Moscow was stiff and bureaucratic, and Bob felt distain for Americans from the Russian officials.

But once through customs, it was a different experience. There to greet him (along with reporters and photographers) were a dozen representatives from the Armenian Writers' Union, who welcomed Bob and embraced the urn. Bob and his group were escorted to a hotel and treated to celebrations and toasting. The next day Bob flew to Armenia, where he was greeted by crowds of admiring people. Saroyan had told the world about Armenia, and his ashes were revered.

His time in Armenia involved nearly non-stop observances and formalities, with the highpoint on Saturday, when the urn was buried in Gomidas Park in downtown Yerevan (the capital of Armenia). The park was packed by around 5,000 people. Government officials made speeches, lavishing praise and admiration on "our beloved William."

Days later, when he returned to Gomidas Park for a last look at Saroyan's tomb, there was a crowd of people praising Saroyan and crying over his grave!

Later, when he reflected on his trip to Armenia, Damir's face broke into a smile. Asked about going so far to do a favor for his friend, he said he had no regrets.

Notes and Sources

Historical San Francisco People

Lillie Coit: The Loves of Miss Lil

Lillie Coit was a unique lady who left San Francisco a beautiful tower, an unusual statue, and many legends. Much of the background information for this story was derived from Holdredge, Helen (1967), *Firebelle Lillie: The life and Times of Lillie Coit of San Francisco.* New York, NY: Meredith Press. Additional details came from Svanevik, Michael and Burgett, Shirley (2002), *Pillars of the Past: At Rest at Cypress Lawn Memorial Park.* Colma, CA; Cypress Lawn Heritage Foundation.

Emperor Norton: Don't Call it Frisco!

I have heard stories about Emperor Norton since I moved to San Francisco, and I suspected that most of them were bogus. It turns out most are true. Sources for this article included: Moylan, Peter. *Emperor Norton, The Encyclopedia of San Francisco,* retrieved from www.sfhistoryencyclopedia.com; Cowen, Robert Ernest. (2000, November 5). *Norton I, Emperor of the United States and Protector of Mexico,* retrieved from www.emperornorton.net/Norton-Cowen; and Andrews, Evan (2014, September 17), *The Strange Case of Emperor Norton I of the United States, Retrieved from* www.history.com.

Friedel Klussmann: The Cable Car Lady

I hadn't heard of Freidel Klussmann until I toured the San Francisco Cable Car Museum, where a wonderful description of this dedicated woman is available to the public. Articles that helped supplement the museum information were: Rice, Walter and Lupiz, Val. *The Cable Car Lady and the Mayor,* retrieved from http://www.sfmuseum.net; and San Francisco History Center, San Francisco Public Library. (2012, August 28). *San Francisco's Cable Car Lady,* retrieved from http://sfhcbasc.blogspot.com.

Adolph Sutro: Building a Legend

The western portion of San Francisco was highly-influenced by this eccentric and generous man. Sources included: Stewart, Robert and Stewart, Mary Frances. (1962). *Adolph Sutro: A Biography.* Berkeley, CA: Howell-North; Holmes, Eugenia Kellogg. (2012). *Adolph Sutro: Brief Story of a Brilliant Life.* San Francisco, CA: Forgotten Books; (2002, January 11). *Adolph Sutro,* retrieved from www.outsidelands.org; and *Adolph Sutro (1830 – 1898),* retrieved from www.americanjerusalem.com.

Joseph Strauss: The Mighty Task is Done

The story behind the man who engineered the Golden Gate Bridge is surprising and inspiring. Sources included: Davis, Mark A.. (1987, May). *The Man With the Golden Gate Bridge,* retrieved from www.magazine.uc.edu; *Biography: Joseph Strauss,* retrieved from www.pbs.org; and (2012, August 24); *Joseph B. Strauss, Golden Gate Bridge Engineer,* rtetrieved from www.artandarchitecture-sf.com.

James Van Ness: A Square and a Street

San Francisco must have been a wild place to live when Van Ness was mayor. Sources for this article included: Nuno, Gregory J., (1993). *A History of Union Square.* published in *The Argonaut*, Taniguchi, Nancy J., (2016). *Dirty Deeds: Land, Violence, and the 1856 San Francisco Vigilance Committee.* Norman, OK: University of Oklahoma Press.; and Nolte, Carl. 2006, August 18. *San Francisco: Recalling the End of the Wild West*, retrieved from www.sfgate.com.

Alma Spreckels: She Got Her Sugar Daddy

San Francisco has had many colorful characters in its past; this was one of the most colorful! Sources included: Scharlach, Bernice. (1990*). Big Alma: San Francisco's Alma Spreckels.* Berkeley, CA: Heyday; Craig, Christopher. *Alma Spreckels: Historical Essa*y, retrieved from http://www.foundsf.org; and Carroll, Jerry. (1995, October 29). *The Palace That Alma Built*, retrieved from www.sfgate.com.

San Francisco and the Arts

Tony Bennett: I Left My Heart

George Cory and Douglass Cross really did leave their hearts in San Francisco, and they moved back to the Bay Area shortly after their song became popular and lived off of the royalties from it the rest of their lives. Sources for this article included Bennett, Tony (with Friedwald, Will). (1998). *The Good Life*. New York, NY: Pocket Books; Bennett, Tony (with Simon, Scott)/ (2016). *Just Getting Started*. New York, NY: HarperCollins; Tony Bennett Biography, retrieved from www.tonybennett.com; and (2016, August 30). Tony Bennett Biography, retrieved from www.biography.com.

Ansel Adams: Visualization

A true California legend, Ansel Adams spent his life following his passion. Today, he influences everyone who loves photography and Yosemite. Sources for this article included: Turnage, William. *Ansel Adams, Photographer*, retrieved from www.anseladams.com; *Ansel Adams – Environmental Activist, Photographer (1902-1984)*, retrieved from www.biography.com; (KPBS). (2002), Burns, Ric. (2002). and *Ansel Adams: A Documentary Film*, retrieved from www.youtube.com. Rights to use the photo of Moon and Half Dome courtesy of Collection Center for Creative Photography, The University of Arizona, ©The Ansel Adams Publishing Rights Trust.

Maya Angelou: The Importance of Courage

What an amazing life this talented and inspirational woman led! Sources included: Angelou, Maya. (1969). *I Know Why the Caged Bird Sings*. New York, NY: Random House; Fernandez, Lisa. *Maya Angelou Was 1st Black, Female San Francisco Street Car Conductor*, retrieved from www.nbcbayarea.com; Sernoffsky, Evan. (2014, May 28). *Maya Angelou's San Francisco Connections*, retrieved from www.sfgate.com; (2104, May 28). *Maya Angelou, Poet and Author Who Got Her Start in Bay Area, Dies at 86*, retrieved from www.sanfrancisco.cbslocal.com; and Allen-Price, Olivia and Brekke, Dan. (2014, May 28). *Maya Angelou: Remembering a Cultural Giant's Life in San Francisco*, retrieved from ww2kqed.org.

Ruth Asawa: Good Comes Through Adversity

Ruth was a very friendly and distinguished Noe Valley neighbor for many years. Sources for this article include Baker, Kenneth. (2013, August 6). *California Sculptor Ruth Asawa Dies.* retrieved from www.sfgate.com, Martin, Douglas. (2013, August 17). *Ruth Asawa, an Artist Who Wove Wire, Dies at 87.* retrieved from www.nytimes.com. Japanese American National Museum. (2007, May 24). *Strength in Beauty: Ruth Asawa.* retrieved from www.discovernikkei.org, Wong-Frentzel, Shirley. (2013, August 29). *Remembering Ruth Asawa.* retrieved from www.sfcmc.org, *Ruth Asawa,* retrieved from www.ruthasawa.com, *Denso Encyclopedia,* retrieved from www.encyclopedia.densho.org.

Michael Tilson Thomas: It's About the Music

MTT has meant so much to so many people in San Francisco, and he has brought so much to our city! Sources for this article included: Tommasini, Anthony. (2014, November 14). *A Boyish Patriarch Leaps Over Boundaries,* retrieved from www.nytimes.com; Duffie, Bruce. (1987, March). *A Conversation with Conductor Michael Tilson Thomas,* retrieved from www.bruceduffie.com; Garchik, Leah. (2014, November 3). *38 Years Together, Tilson Thomas and Robison Marry,* retrieved from www.sfgate.com; and Ewers, Justin. (2008, November 19). *America's Best Leaders: Michael Tilson Thomas,* San Francisco Symphony.

Richard Serra: The Language of Art

It is easy to admire someone who spends his life pursuing his passion, which is how I felt about Richard Serra after studying his life story. Sources included two wonderful interviews with Charlie Rose in 2001 and 2007 retrieved from www.youtube.com; *Richard Serra Biography, Art, and Analysis of Works,* retrieved from www.theartstory.org; *Richard Serra: American, 1938, San Francisco, California: Biography,* retrieved from www.sfmoma.org; Simmons, Mark. *Richard Serra: The Coagula Interview,* retrieved from www.coagula.com.

Michael de Young: The Power of Information

The story of the name behind the de Young museum is inspiring and peculiar. Sources included: Brechin, Gray. *Michael de Young: Unfinished History,* retrieved from www.foundsf.org; *M.H. de Young and Charles de Young,* retrieved from www.norcalmediamuseum.org; and *The Maritime Heritage Project. Ship Passengers: Sea Captains,* retrieved from wwws.shippassengers.com

San Francisco Politicos

"Sunny Jim" Rolph: A Self-Made Man

There were three primary sources for the background information about James Rolph. Foremost, an article written by Gladys Hansen, located in The Virtual Museum of the City of San Francisco, which supplied basic information. Other sources included Crafts, Daniel Steven, *Mayor "Sunny Jim" Rolph,* retrieved from *www.foundsf.org.* Worthen, James. (2006). *Governor James Rolph and the Great Depression in California,* Jefferson, NC: McFarland and Company.

Joe Alioto: A Beautiful Building

Researching this flamboyant and controversial San Francisco personality was an intriguing task. Three sources helped immensely: *Time Magazine.* (1972, November 13). *Alioto's Odyssey.* retrieved from http://content.time.com; Ryder, Clyde D. *A Legacy to Leave Aside: Joseph Alioto, San Francisco Mayor.* retrieved from www.academic.edu; and Williams, Lance and Hatfield, Larry D., (1998, January 30). *Joseph Alioto 1916 – 1998*, retrieved from http://www.sfgate.com.

Willie Brown: Da Mayor's Inauguration

Da Mayor has been a favorite of mine since I moved to San Francisco, and it was fun writing about him. He was sworn in as mayor of San Francisco January 8, 1996 by Superior Court Judge John Dearman, a former law partner of Brown. Sources for this article included: Brown, Willie (2008). *Basic Brown: My Life and Our Times.* New York, NY: Simon & Schuster; Stevens, Elizabeth Lesly. (2012, July/August). *The Power Broker.* retrieved from http://www.washingtonmonthly.com; Richardson, James. (1996). *Willie Brown: A Biography.* Berkeley, CA: University of California Press; and Willie Brown Biography – Academy of Achievement. (July 13, 2010), retrieved from www.achievement.org.

George Moscone: An Extraordinary City

George Moscone is one of the reasons San Francisco is such an interesting place to live. He was a good man whose life ended too soon. Sources for this article included: Nolte, Carl. (2003, November 26). *City Hall Slayings, 25 Years Later,* retrieved from www.sfgate.com.; and Gazis-Sax, Joel. (1996). *The Martyrdom of Mayor George Moscone,* retrieved from www.notfrisco.com.

Harvey Milk: Give Them Hope

While I've heard about Harvey since I moved to San Francisco I knew very little about his life, and I was surprised to learn he was closeted during his early years. His story is inspiring, and I thank Randy Shilts for telling it in such a captivating and straight-forward manner. Much of the background information for this article came from Randy's masterpiece: Shiltz, Randy. (1982). *The Mayor of Castro Street: The Life and Times of Harvey Milk. New York NY:* St. Martin's Press. Other sources include: *The Official Harvey Milk Biography,* retrieved from www.milkfoundation.org; Cloud, John. (1999, June 14). *The Pioneer Harvey Milk, retrieved from http://content.time.com; Harvey Milk.* (2015), retrieved from www.biography.com; and Popovic, Srdja and Miller, Matthew. (2015, February 5). *Harvey Milk's First Crusade: Dog Poop,* retrieved from www.politico.com.

Dianne Feinstein: Back to Work

It's easy to admire someone who has dedicated her entire life to serving her country and I found my admiration for Senator Feinstein increasing as I researched her life story. Much of the information for this article can be attributed to two sources: the wonderful biography of Feinstein: Roberts, Jerry. (1994). *Diane Feinstein: Never Let Them See You Cry.* New York, NY: HarperCollins; and a heart-breaking video interview with Senator Feinstein on YouTube and summarized in *The San Francisco Chronicle,* Gordon, Rachel. (2008, November 26). *Feinstein Recalls S.F.'s "Day of Infamy,"* retrieved from http://www.sfgate.com. The two men with Feinstein in the illustration are her long-time aide, Peter Nardoza (behind her), and San Francisco Police Chief, Charles Gain (beside her).

Ed Lee: Worth Every Sacrifice

Ed Lee was an honorable man and caring mayor, and San Francisco was fortunate to have had him work on their behalf. Sources for this article include: Background information about the mayor came from his website: *About the Mayor*, retrieved from www.sfmayor.org; Nevius, C.W. (2016, November 3), *Public Housing Hits Home with Mayor Lee*, retrieved from www.sfchronicle.com; Serwer, Andy. (2013, December 11), *Everyman Ed Lee*, in *Fortune Magazine*. retrieved from *www.fortune.com*; Steinberg, Jon. (2015, March 31). *Lunch with the Lees, retrieved from www.modernluxury.com;* and SF Neighbor Alliance for Ed Lee for Mayor. (2011). *The Ed Lee Story: An Unexpected Mayo*r.

San Francisco Writers

Mark Twain: Out with the Comet

No one writes dialog like Mark Twain! Background information for this article came from *The Official Web Site of Mark Twain*, retrieved from www.cmgww.com; (2006, July 5); Loving, Jerome. (2010). *Mark Twain: The Adventures of Samuel Clemens. Berkeley, CA:* University of California Press; and Smith, Harriet Elinor, Editor; (2010). *Autobiography of Mark Twain, Volume 1. Berkeley, CA:* University of California Press; (1962). *Roughing It.* New York, NY: Harper & Row; and (2015, October 9) *How Mark Twain Got Fired in San Francisco*, Kamiya, Gary, retrieved from www.sfchronicle.com.

Ina Coolbrith: The Saving Power of Poetry

I was unaware of the impact of this remarkable woman until I ran across her in Ben Tarnoff's book about San Francisco writers called *The Bohemians*. New York, NY: The Penguin Press (2014). I found her again in George Rathmell's book called *Realms of Gold*. Berkeley, CA: Creative Book Company; (1998). Still wanting to know more, I turned to Aleta George's biography titled *Ina Coolbrith: The Bittersweet Song of California's First Poet Laureate*. Shifting Plates Press; (2015). My sincere appreciation to all three authors for helping keep Ina's story alive!

Jack London: Left a Treasure Trove

I fell for the Valley of the Moon and Jack London's writing when I first moved to San Francisco. Sources for this article included: *The Jack London Online Collection*, Jean and Charles Schulz Information Center, Sonoma State University. retrieved from www.london.sonoma.edu.; (2013, June), *Who Was Jack London; An Overview,* retrieved from www.getyourwordsworth.com; Hari, Johann. (2010, August). *Jack London's Dark Side*, retrieved from www.slate.com; (2015, January). *The World of Jack London: Jack London Biography*, retrieved from www.jacklondons.net; and Asprey, Matthew (Editor). (2010). *Jack London San Francisco Stories.* Sydney, Australia: Sydney Samizdat Press.

Dashiell Hammett: One of the Tough Guys

Dashiell Hammett is one of my favorite "hard-boiled" authors, and he is the inspiration behind the Dashiell Hammett Society of Studs (DHSOS), of which I am an officer. Sources for this article included: Hamlin, Jesse. (2005, February 7). *Dashiell Hammett's legacy lies not only in his writing, but in his living — rough, wild and on the edge,* retrieved from www.sfgate.com; Hammett, Jo. (2001). *Dashiell Hammett: A*

Daughter Remembers. New York NY: Carroll & Graf Publishers; Stroby, Wallace. (2015, July 8). *The Great American Mystery Writer*, retrieved from www.wallacestroby.com; Layman, Richard and Rivett, Julie M. (editors). *Selected Letters of Dashiell Hammett: 1921-1960*, retrieved from *www.nytimes.com*; and Hammett, Dashiell. (1992). *The Maltese Falcon*, New York, NY: Vintage Books.

William Saroyan: Determined to be a Writer

"Bill" Saroyan was an excellent writer and a complicated man. Sources for this article included: Lee, Lawrence and Gifford, Barry. (1984). *Saroyan: A Biography*. New York, NY: Harper & Row; Darwent, Brian. (1983, November). *A Biographical Sketch Based Largely on His Own Writings*, retrieved from www.williamsaroyansociety.org; *William Saroyan: A Brief Biography*, retrieved from www.dickinson.edu; and *William Saroyan*, retrieved from www.britannica.com.

Lawrence Ferlinghetti: One Fine Day!

I had the good fortune to have dinner with Lawrence a few years ago, and I enjoyed meeting and talking with San Francisco's premier poet. Background information about Lawrence Ferlinghetti's life came from *A Brief Biography of Lawrence Ferlinghetti* on City Lights Bookstore's website, retrieved from www.city-lights.com and Guthrie, Julian. (2012, September 24). *Lawrence Ferlinghetti's Indelible Image, The San Francisco Chronicle*. The three poems are taken from Mr. Ferlinghetti's book: Ferlinghetti, Lawrence. (2001). *San Francisco Poems*, San Francisco, CA, City Lights Foundation.

Herb Caen: Part of San Francisco's Everyday Life

I was one of those readers who went to Herb's column first each morning. Sources for this article included: Conrad, Barnaby. (1997). *The World of Herb Caen: 1938 – 1997*. San Francisco, CA: The Chronicle Publishing Company; Caen, Herb. (1997). *Herb Caen's San Francisco: 1976 – 1991*. San Francisco, CA: Chronicle Books; (2015, March 26). *Herb Caen Archive, The San Francisco Chronicle*, retrieved from www.sfgate.com; Ybarra, Michael. (1997, February 2). *Herb Caen, 80, San Francisco Voice, Dies*, retrieved from www.nytimes.com; and Gross, Jane. (1993, May 26). *At Lunch With: Herb Caen; Romancing San Francisco in 1,000 Words or Less*, retrieved from www.nytimes.com.

Carl Nolte: News Doesn't Happen in the Office

I have read and admired Carl Nolte for many years, and he has inspired my writing. Sources include Nolte, Carl. (2005). *The San Francisco Century: A City Rises from the Ruins of the 1906 Earthquake and Fire*. San Francisco, CA: The San Francisco Chronicle Publishing; Nolte, Carl. (2015, March 31). *Native Son – Carl Nolte on San Francisco*, retrieved from www.sfgate.com; (2015, March 31). *Carl Nolte: Columnist*. retrieved from www.sfchronicle.com; Wilson, Yumi. (2009, March 30). *Carl Nolte*. retrieved from www.youtube.com.

The Summer of Love

Peter Coyote: Love, Power, and Wisdom

It's easy to admire this man who survived the Summer of Love and emerged as a successful activist, author, actor, and academic. Sources included: Coyote, Peter. (1998). Sleeping Where I Fall. Berkeley, CA:

Coyote, Peter. (2007, May 20). Summer of Love: 40 Years Later, retrieved from www.sfgate.com; Counterpoint; Biography, retrieved from www.petercoyote.com; (2009, August 28). *Where the Counterculture Prevails*, retrieved from www.youtube.com; Talbot, David. (2012). *Season of the Witch*. New York, NY: Free Press; and (2016, March 25), and David Talbot in Conversation with Peter Coyote at the Contemporary Jewish Museum, retrieved from www.youtube.com.

Bill Graham: Laughter, Love, and Music

Bill Graham led an inspirational life, and he helped many people (especially young musicians) get their lives together. Sources included: Greenfield, Robert. *Who Was Bill Graham*, retrieved from www.billgrahamfoundation.org; Lambert, Bruce. (1991, October 27). *Bill Graham, Rock Impresario, Dies at 60 in Crash*, retrieved from www.nytimes.com; *Bill Graham and the Rock & Roll Revolution*, retrieved from www.skirball.org; Ankeny, Jason. *Artist Biography: Bill Graham*; retrieved from www.allmusic.com; and Talbot, David. (2012). *Season of the Witch*. New York, NY: Free Press.

Janis Joplin: Do One Thing Well

There were three major sources of information for this story about a very talented woman who led a very sad life. They are: Echols, Alice. (1999). *Scars of Sweet Paradise: The Life and Times of Janis Joplin*: New York: Metropolitan Books/Henry Holt and Company; Angel, Ann. (2010), *Janis Joplin: Rise Up Singing*. New York, NY: Abrams Books; and Talbot, David. (2012). *Season of the Witch*. New York, NY: Free Press. Additional background information came from Weller, Sheila. (2015, November 27). *Discovering the Vulnerable Woman Behind Janis Joplin's Legend*, retrieved from www.vanityfair.com.; and interviews between Janis Joplin and Dick Cavett on www.youtube.com.

Jerry Garcia: I Play for My Life

He affected many lives and left a treasure trove of music. Sources included: Jackson, Blair. (1999). *Garcia: An American Life*. New York, NY: Penguin Books; McNally, Dennis. (2002). *A Long Strange Trip*. New York, NY: Broadway Books; Talbot, David. (2012). *Season of the Witch*. New York, NY: Free Press; and Gilmore, Mikal. (1995, September 21). *Jerry Garcia: 1942-1995*, retrieved from www.rollingstone.com.

Grace Slick: One Thing at a Time

What a group! What a voice! Sources for this article include: Jefferson Airplane Website, *Grace Slick*, retrieved from www.jeffersonairplane.com; Selvin, Joel. (2007, May 20). *Summer of Love: 40 Years Later/Grace Slick*, retrieved from www.sfgate.com; Fong-Torres, Ben. (1970, November 12). *Grace Slick with Paul Kantner: The Rolling Stone Interview*, retrieved from www.rollingstone.com; Millar, Aaron. (2017, May 21). Golden Daze: 50 Years on from the Summer of Love, retrieved from www.theguardian.com; and Talbot, David. (2012). *Season of the Witch*. New York, NY: Free Press.

Carlos Santana: Helping the World Heal

Two of my all-time favorite musical albums are by Carlos Santana: *Santana*, produced in 1969 and *Supernatural*, from 1999. Carlos Santana is a remarkable musician with wide-ranging appeal and staying power. Sources included: Santana, Carlos. (2014). *The Universal Tone*. New York, NY: Little, Brown and Company;

Shapiro, Marc. (2000). *Carlos Santana: Back on Top*. New York, NY: St. Martin's Press; Carlos Santana: *Biography*, retrieved from www.santana.com; and Heath, Chris. (2000, March 16). *The Epic Life of Carlos Santana*, retrieved from www.rollingstone.com.

San Francisco at Play

Joe DiMaggio: The End of the Streak
I do volunteer work across the street from a playground named after this remarkable athlete, so I have frequent opportunity to reminisce on his legacy. Sources for this article include: Cramer, Richard Ben. (2000). *Joe DiMaggio: The Hero's Life*. New York NY: Simon & Schuster; Seidel, Michael. (2002). *Streak: Joe DiMaggio and the Summer of '41*. New York NY: McGraw-Hill; Rosenstock, Barb. (2014). *The Streak: How Joe DiMaggio Became America's Hero*. Honesdale, PA: Calkins Creek; The Virtual Museum of the City of San Francisco. *Joe DiMaggio, the Yankee Clippe*, retrieved from www.sfmuseum.net; Stark, Jason. (2011, May 15). *Baseball's Unbreakable Recor*, retrieved from www.sports.espn.go.com.

Willie Mays: Kept His Cool
Willie threw an autographed baseball into the stands during the final game at Candlestick Park. I caught and still have that ball, which reminds me of all that Willie Mays did for baseball and San Francisco. This article is a tribute to him. Sources for this article included: Hirsch, James S. (2011). *Willie Mays: The Life, the Legend*, New York, NY: Scribner; Mays, Willie. 1966. *Willie Mays: My Life In and Out of Baseball*. New York, NY: E. P. Dutton & Co.; Linge, Mary Kay. (2005). *Willie Mays: A Biography*. Westport, CT: Greenwood Press; *Willie Mays' Embarrassing Introduction to S.F*, retrieved from www.sfgate.com; Ostler, Scott (2011, May 6); *How Mays Went from Outsider to the No. 1 Giant*, retrieved from www.sfgate.com; Shea, John (2009, March 8); *When Willie Wasn't Welcome*, retrieved from www.eichlernetwork.com.

Joe Montana: Mr. Big Game
When we watched the 49ers during those fabulous years of dominance, we knew that somehow Joe Montana would find a way to help them win. Joe was a pleasure to watch and to write about. Sources included Zimmerman, Paul. (1989, January 30). *Joe COOL*, retrieved from Sports Illustrated website at www.si.com; Shea, John. (2016, January 25). *Super Bowl XXIII: Montana at His Cool Best in Drive for the Ages*, retrieved from www.sfgate.com; Schwartz, Larry. *Montana was Comeback King*, retrieved at www.espn.go.com; *Joe Montana – Athlete, Football Player*, retrieved from www.biography.com; (1989, January 22). *Montana Drives 49ers Past Bengals in Super Bowl XXIII*, retrieved from www.49erswebzone.com.

Johnny Miller: Golfing Nirvana
Johnny Miller was one of the most accurate iron players of all time, and he has been an interesting and honest TV commentator. I used four primary sources for this article: Diaz, Jaime. (2010, October 18). *The Genius of Johnny*, retrieved from www.golfdigest.com; Frakes, Bill. (1982, March). *Golf Magazine Interview: Johnny Miller*, retrieved from www.golf.com; *Johnny Miller*, retrieved from www.worldgolfhalloffame.org; *Johnny Miller – U.S.A. – Biography of His Golfing Career*, retrieved from www.sporting-heroes.net

Alice Marble: A Story for the Ages

Three sources supplied much of the background for the story about this remarkable and largely unknown woman: Marble, Alice and Leatherman, Dale. (1991). *Courting Danger*. New York, NY: St. Martin's Press; *Alice Marble. (2015). The Biography.com website.* Retrieved from *http://www.biography.com;* and Ungaretti, Lorri. *A Remarkable Life: Alice Marble*, retrieved from http://www.sfcityguides.org/public_guidelines.html.

Jim Corbett: Gentleman Jim

This native San Franciscan, banker, and member of the Olympic Club developed a new and innovative style of boxing that is still used today. Sources for this article included *International Boxing Hall of Fame, James J. Corbett*, retrieved from www.ibhof.com; *Eyewitness to History, "Gentleman Jim" Corbett Knocks Out John L. Sullivan, 1892*, retrieved from nwww.eyewitnesstohistory.com; Corbishley, Sam. (2017, February 18). *On This Day: Boxing Pioneer James J. Corbett Passes Away Aged 66*, retrieved from www.boxingnewson-line.net; Cox, Monte. *James J. Corbett, "Turning Point in Pugilism"*, retrieved from www.coxcorner.tripod.com.

In Their Own Way

Cleve Jones: The Movement

When I heard Cleve speak at a book signing event, I was inspired to help carry on the fight for equal rights. Sources for this article include: Jones, Cleve. (2016). *When We Rise*. New Your, NY: Hachette Book Group; Teeman, Tim. (2017, February 22). *Cleve Jones on Harvey Milk, "When We Rise," and Fighting for LGBT Equality Under Trump*, retrieved from www.thedailybeast.com; Jones, Kevin L. (2017), February 27). *Cleve Jones on "When We Rise" and the Power of Activism*, retrieved from ww2.kqed.org; and a terrific interview on Fresh Air (NPR). (2016, November 29). *LGBTQ Activist Cleve Jones: 'I'm Well Aware How Fragile Life Is'*, retrieved from www.youtube.com.

Carol Doda: A Good Time

Carol was a legend when I moved to San Francisco, well-known to tourists and locals alike. Sources for this article included Guthrie, Julian. (2011, October 20). *Ex-stripper Carol Doda Reflects on Career, Singing*, retrieved from www.sfgate.com; Fagan, Kevin and Whiting, Sam. (2015, November 11). *Legendary S. F. Stripper Carol Doda Dies at 78*, retrieved from www.sfgate.com; Roberts, Sam. (2015, November 11). *Carol Doda, Pioneer of Topless Entertainment, Dies at 78*, retrieved from www.nytimes.com; and Nicolini, Kim. (2015, November 16). *The Myth of the Perfect 36: What I Learned About Stripping and Life From Carol Doda*, retrieved from www.counterpunch.com.

Don Novello: Father Guido Sarducci

Father Guido Sarducci was a favorite character on *Saturday Night Live* in the 1970s and 1980s, and it was fun researching, writing about, and talking to his creator. Two sources that were especially helpful were: Benson, Heidi (2003, September 18). *Don Novello's a man of many words, whether he's Father Guido Sarducci, scribbler Lazlo Toth, or even a political candidate*, The San Francisco Chronicle, retrieved from http://www.sfgate.com; and Novello, Don. (1992, January 7). *The Lazio Letters*, New York, NY, Workman Publishing Company.

Don Herron: Shadowing Dashiell Hammett

I was fortunate to join Don for his Dashiell Hammett tour — thank you, Don! Don Herron's book is: Herron, Don. (2009). *The Dashiell Hammett Tour: Thirtieth Anniversary Guidebook.* San Francisco, CA: Vince Emery Productions.

Lee Roberson: They Will Always be His Kids

Lee Roberson has been an inspiration to me and to the hundreds of kids he has helped over the years. In 2015, the gymnasium where he spent so many years working with his kids was rightly named after him.

Bob Damir: A Very Special Favor

I met Bob Damir at an Armenian Church fundraiser when he sat at our table, found out I was a writer, and told me he had a story to tell. This was his story. I interviewed him, wrote his story, and his wife read it to him as he lay dying. He told her I got it "exactly right." Thank you, Bob!

PHOTOGRAPHY CREDITS

Page 6   View of San Francisco from Sanchez Hill. Photo by Dale Fehringer, 2018.

Page 8   San Francisco from the top of Twin Peaks. Photo by Dale Fehringer, 2018.

Page 21   The Golden Gate Bridge. Photo by Dale Fehringer, 2018.

Page 26   San Francisco's Legion of Honor Museum. Photo by Dale Fehringer, 2018.

Page 30   Statue of Tony Bennett in front of San Francisco's Fairmont Hotel. Photo by Dale Fehringer, 2018.

Page 35   *Moon and Half Dome, Yosemite National Park, California,* 1960. Photograph by Ansel Adams. (c) The Ansel Adams Publishing Rights Trust

Page 41   Ruth Asawa wire sculptures at San Francisco's de Young Museum. Photo by Dale Fehringer, 2018.

Page 47   Richard Serra's *Sequence,* at the time located at San Francisco Museum of Modern Art, now located On Stanford University's Palo Alto campus. Photo by Dale Fehringer, 2018.

Page 51   San Francisco's de Young Museum. Photo by Dale Fehringer, 2018.

Page 52   San Francisco's City Hall. Photo by Dale Fehringer, 2018.

Page 68   The "Painted Ladies" at San Francisco's Alamo Square. Photo by Dale Fehringer, 2018.

Page 92   Tribute to the Summer of Love at San Francisco's Conservatory of Flowers. Photo by Dale Fehringer, 2018.

Page 106   Willie Mays statue in front of San Francisco's Oracle Park. Photo by Dale Fehringer, 2019.

Page 120   San Francisco's Castro District. Photo by Dale Fehringer, 2018.

ILLUSTRATION CREDITS

We hope you enjoyed the illustrations. Creating art with computer software is not new, but its use in transforming historic photographs is becoming a trend.

Every attempt was made to adhere to copyright rules while creating the illustrations for this book. In some cases one or more photographs that are in the public domain were used to inspire an illustration. In those instances it was not necessary to obtain permission to use the photograph(s). In other cases, one or more photographs that inspired an illustration had copyrights, and in those cases we went to great efforts to locate the original photographer(s) or agencies and to obtain permission to use the photographs. Still other illustrations were created using inspiration from bits and pieces of various historic photographs, paintings, videos, and/or television footage and then significantly altering the pieces. In those cases, the result is a montage that relates only peripherally to the original works, and it would have been difficult and inappropriate to try to identify copyright holders and secure permission.

If you would like to see more of John's work or talk to him about it, feel free to contact him at www.mile-stonegallery.com.

Historical San Francisco People

Lillie Coit: The Loves of Miss Lil
This a classic image of Lillie Coit in an old-fashioned dress with a fireman's helmet and her Engine #5 badge. The original photograph, which was taken around 1863, is at the San Francisco Public Library. It is in the public domain. John added modern day Telegraph Hill and the Coit Tower, which was built with funds Lillie left in her will for San Francisco.

Emperor Norton: Don't Call it Frisco!
John started with this classic early 1900's photo of the Emperor dressed in his finest (the photograph is located at the Bancroft Library at U.S. Berkeley and is in the public domain). He created his version of the image and added an umbrella, because it has been reported that the Emperor twirled an umbrella while he walked the streets of San Francisco.

Friedel Klussmann: The Cable Car Lady
The photograph that inspired this image shows Mrs. Klussmann triumphantly leaning out of a cable car after they had been saved. It was taken in 1947 and is courtesy of San Francisco Chronicle/Polaris Images: 05443452 Clem Albers/San Francisco Chronicle/Polaris. John added the modern high-rise building and American flag in the background.

Adolph Sutro: Building a Legend

This illustration stems from a photograph of Adolph Sutro taken around 1885. The original photograph is on the website of the National Park Service (www.nps.gov) and is in the public domain. John adapted the image using computer software, softened Sutro's looks, and added the Sutro Baths and Cliff House.

Joseph Strauss: The Mighty Task is Done

The photograph that influenced this illustration was taken by Peter Stackpole, a well-known and award-winning photojournalist who had a long and brilliant career photographing Hollywood stars, nature settings, and construction of bridges. His work was featured on the covers of numerous *Life Magazines*. The photograph was used here courtesy of Mr. Stackpole's daughter, Kathie Stackpole Bunnell.

James Van Ness: A Square and a Street

The photograph of a stern-looking James Van Ness that was the impetus behind this illustration is included in the online collection of San Francisco mayors on the website of the San Francisco Public Library (www.sfpl.org). It was taken around 1855 and is in the public domain.

Alma Spreckels: She Got Her Sugar Daddy

The photograph that influenced this illustration was taken in 1904 and is in the public domain. At the time the photo was taken Alma de Bretteville was 23, single, working as a model, and searching for a "sugar daddy."

San Francisco and the Arts

Tony Bennett: I Left My Heart

The photograph of Tony Bennett that caught John's eye and influenced this illustration was taken by Maurice Zeldman in 1978. With his brother, Seymour Zeldman, Maurice formed the "Maurice Seymour" studio and took stunning black-and-white photographs of dancers and musicians in the 1930s through the 1960s (with a special focus on ballet dancers). John started with the photograph and used computer programs to create his interpretation of it. The photograph is courtesy of © Maurice Seymour/mptvimages.com.

Ansel Adams: Visualization

J. Malcom Greany, a well-known nature photographer, took the photograph of Ansel Adams around 1950 that inspired John's illustration. It shows a young Ansel Adams and his camera, preparing to take a photograph of Yosemite. Greany was a friend of Adams' and a photographer for the U.S. Army when he took this photo. Because Greany was working for the U.S. Government when he took the photograph, it is in the public domain.

San Francisco Politicos

"Sunny Jim" Rolph: A Self-Made Man
The photograph behind this illustration was taken in the 1920s while Rolph was mayor of San Francisco. It is in the public domain.

Joe Alioto: A Beautiful Building
The photograph that influenced this illustration was taken February 26, 1973 in Mayor Alioto's office in San Francisco's City Hall. It is used here courtesy of the Associated Press (AP Photo: 730226064).

Harvey Milk: Give Them Hope
The photograph that inspired this illustration of San Francisco Supervisor Harvey Milk was taken in 1977. It is courtesy of the Associated Press (AP Photo: 060621030869).

Dianne Feinstein: Back to Work
The iconic photograph behind this illustration of San Francisco Acting Mayor Dianne Feinstein with Police Chief Charles Gain (left) and aide Peter Nardoza was taken November 28, 1978, shortly after Mayor George Moscone and Supervisor Harvey Milk were killed by former Supervisor Dan White. It is courtesy of the Associated Press (AP Photo: 7811280424).

Ed Lee: Worth Every Sacrifice
The photograph that John used to influence this illustration was taken by San Francisco photographer Myleen Hollero (www. http://myleenhollero.com) in 2011. She photographed Mayor Lee many times and gave her generous permission to use this one.

San Francisco Writers

Mark Twain: Out with the Comet
The photograph of Samuel Clemens (Mark Twain) that influenced John's illustration was taken at the height of his career, around 1904. It is in the public domain.

Ina Coolbrith: The Saving Power of Poetry
The photograph that gave John the idea for this illustration is located at the Oakland Public Library where Ina was head librarian for many years. The photograph was taken around 1870 when Ina was 29 or 30. It is in the public domain.

Jack London: Left a Treasure Trove
The photograph behind this illustration was taken by Jack London's wife, Charmian, aboard their ship (the Roamer) in 1914. The photograph is located in the Sonoma County Library and is in the public domain.

Herb Caen: Part of San Francisco's Everyday Life

This is a classic Herb Caen pose, with his arms on his beloved Royal typewriter. The photograph that inspired John's illustration is courtesy of San Francisco Chronicle/Polaris Images: 05424636 Gary Fong/San Francisco Chronicle/Polaris.

Carl Nolte: News Doesn't Happen in the Office

The photograph behind John's illustration of Carl Nolte is courtesy of San Francisco Chronicle/Polaris Images: 06355672 Mike Kepka/San Francisco Chronicle/Polaris.

The Summer of Love

Peter Coyote: Love, Power, and Wisdom

The idea for this illustration of a thoughtful Peter Coyote came from a photograph on Peter's website (http://www.petercoyote.com/bwphotos.html). It is used with his permission.

Janis Joplin: Do One Thing Well

The photograph that inspired this illustration of Janis Joplin was taken in October 1970. It is courtesy of the Associated Press (AP Photo: 701001057).

Grace Slick: One Thing at a Time

The photograph behind this illustration of Jefferson Airplane singer Grace Slick was taken in 1970. It is used courtesy of the Associated Press (AP Photo: 70010113810).

Carlos Santana: Helping the World Heal

There have been many phases of the life and career of Carlos Santana. The photo that was the stimulus for this illustration was taken May 17, 1999, just as his career was taking off again, due to the popularity of his "Supernatural" album. It is courtesy of the Associated Press (AP Photo: 99051701908).

San Francisco at Play

Joe DiMaggio: The End of the Streak

The photograph behind this illustration of San Francisco native, Joe DiMaggio, was taken in 1946. It is courtesy of the Associated Press (AP Photo: 460306025).

Willie Mays: Kept His Cool

This illustration of San Francisco Giants star outfielder Willie Mays was stimulated by a photograph taken in 1962. It is courtesy of the Associated Press (AP Photo: 620301065).

Joe Montana: Mr. Big Game

This illustration of San Francisco 49ers star quarterback Joe Montana was prompted by a photograph taken by Peter Read Miller in 1984. It is courtesy of the Associated Press (AP Photo: 63782179144).

Johnny Miller: Golfing Nirvana

The idea for this illustration stemmed from a photograph of golfing legend Johnny Miller taken at the first tee during the British Open in July, 1976. It is courtesy of the Associated Press (AP Photo: 760710019).

Alice Marble: A Story for the Ages

The impetus for this illustration of American tennis player Alice Marble was a photograph taken June 17, 1939 at the conclusion of the Kent All Comers Championship Cup in Kent, England. It is courtesy of the Associated Press (AP Photo: 390617064).

Jim Corbett: Gentleman Jim

The photograph of Jim Corbett behind this illustration was taken at the height of Corbett's career in the 1880s. It is in the public domain.

In Their Own Way

Cleve Jones: The Movement

The photograph that gave John the inspiration for this illustration of Cleve Jones was taken in 2008. It is used courtesy of San Francisco Chronicle/Polaris Images: 05302389 David Miller/AbacaUSA/Polaris.

Don Novello: Father Guido Sarducci

The photograph that prompted this illustration was taken in 1986. John used computer software to soften it and add a scarf. It is used here with the generous permission of Pat Johnson (www.patjohnson.com), who has been a successful photographer in the music, sports, and entertainment industries for over 25 years. ©Pat Johnson.

Don Herron: Shadowing Dashiell Hammett

This illustration was influenced by a photograph on Don Herron's website (www.donherron.com/the-tour/current-walks). It is used here with his permission.

Lee Roberson: They Will Always be His Kids

This illustration was inspired by a photograph of a young and vibrant Lee Roberson. It was provided by his family, who gave their permission to use it here.

Bob Damir: A Very Special Favor

The idea for this illustration was a photograph of Bob carrying the urn containing half of William Saroyan's ashes as he debarked from a long and arduous flight to the Soviet Union. It was provided by Bob and used with permission of his wife, Margie.

ACKNOWLEDGEMENTS

Writing a book is a solitary experience. Publishing a book, on the other hand, is a group effort, and there were many people who contributed to this book. To John Milestone, who created the illustrations and cover art, your talents and friendship are greatly appreciated; thank you for hanging in there through a long, and sometimes frustrating process. To Julia Scannell, a wonderful friend and artist, thank you very much for designing the cover. To Lois Pryor, who inspired me and helped design and edit various drafts, thank you for your patience. To Michael Creedman, June Huwa, Judy Dickens, Sue Doyle, Cheryl Chester, Ina Hausner, Kathleen Kokezas, and Terri Wolff — thank you for reviewing and commenting on early versions of the stories. To Tania Cogan, who proof-read and edited the book, thank you for your help and guidance. To the talented and dedicated authors who wrote the books and articles that inspired these stories (see Notes and Sources section), thank you for the treasures you created for us. To the photographers see Illustration Credits) who captured the subjects at crucial times in their lives, thank you for your artistry. To the subjects of the stories, I know it's hard to read about yourself, so thank you for reviewing and commenting on your stories. And, to Patty McCrary, my best friend and the love of my life – thank you for your support and perseverance.

ABOUT THE AUTHOR

Dale Fehringer is a free-lance writer and editor. He has written and edited articles, books, reports, newsletters, marketing material, and training programs, and he is a frequent contributor to *inTravel Magazine* and Storyhouse.org. Dale lives in San Francisco with his wife, Patty. He can be reached at dalefehringer@hotmail.com

ABOUT THE ILLUSTRATOR

J. Arthur Milestone is a fourth-generation San Franciscan and artist. John creates California landscapes and murals for public spaces. You can reach him online or see more of his work at www.MilestoneGallery.com

ABOOKS

ALIVE Book Publishing and ALIVE Publishing Group
are imprints of Advanced Publishing LLC,
3200 A Danville Blvd., Suite 204, Alamo, California 94507

Telephone: 925.837.7303
alivebookpublishing.com